Virtual Arguments

On the Design of Argument Assistants
for Lawyers and Other Arguers

For other titles in the Series see p. 162

INFORMATION TECHNOLOGY & LAW SERIES 6

VIRTUAL ARGUMENTS

On the Design of Argument Assistants for Lawyers and Other Arguers

Bart Verheij

Assistant Professor, Artificial Intelligence Department
University of Groningen

T·M·C·ASSER PRESS
The Hague

The *Information Technology & Law Series* is published
for ITeR by T·M·C·ASSER PRESS
P.O. Box 16163, 2500 BD The Hague, The Netherlands
<www.asserpress.nl>

T·M·C·ASSER PRESS English language books are distributed exclusively by:

Cambridge University Press, The Edinburgh Building, Shaftesbury Road,
Cambridge CB2 2RU, UK,
or
for customers in the USA, Canada and Mexico:
Cambridge University Press, 40 West 20th Street, New York, NY 10011-4211, USA

<www.cambridge.org>

The *Information Technology & Law Series* is an initiative of IT*e*R, the National Programme for Information Technology and Law, which is a research programme set up by the Dutch government and the Netherlands Organisation for Scientific Research (NWO) in The Hague. Since 1995 IT*e*R has published all of its research results in its own book series. In 2002 IT*e*R launched the present internationally orientated and English language *Information Technology & Law Series*. This series deals with the implications of information technology for legal systems and institutions. It is not restricted to publishing IT*e*R's research results. Hence, authors are invited and encouraged to submit their manuscripts for inclusion. Manuscripts and related correspondence can be sent to the Series' Editorial Office, which will also gladly provide more information concerning editorial standards and procedures.

Editorial Office
NWO / IT*e*R
P.O. Box 93461
2509 AL The Hague, The Netherlands
Tel. +31(0)70-3440950; Fax +31(0)70-3832841
E-mail: <iter@nwo.nl>
Web site: <www.nwo.nl/iter>

Single copies or Standing Order
The books in the *Information Technology & Law Series* can either be purchased as single copies or through a standing order. For ordering information see the information on top of this page or visit the publisher's web site at <www.asserpress.nl/cata/itlaw6/fra.htm>.

ISBN 90-6704-190-4
ISSN 1570-2782

Cover and lay-out: Oasis Productions, Nieuwerkerk a/d IJssel, The Netherlands

PREFACE

This book provides an overview of research into the design of argumentation software. The focus is on defeasible argumentation as it occurs in the law. This book reports on interdisciplinary research, and I hope that not only researchers in the field of artificial intelligence and law, but also legal theorists, argumentation theorists and interested lawyers will be able to find their way through the material.

The research was funded by IT*e*R, the National Programme for Law and Information Technology (project numbers 014-37-112 and 014-38-708) and was carried out at the Faculty of Law of the Universiteit Maastricht. I would like to thank Jaap Hage and Bram Roth for their comments on a draft of this text. Earlier versions of much of the material in this book have been presented elsewhere, mostly in workshops and conferences (see the references in the text). An abridged and adapted version of the text, entitled 'Artificial argument assistants for defeasible argumentation', has been published in *Artificial Intelligence*, in a special issue on artificial intelligence and law (Verheij 2003b).

Groningen, September 2004 Bart VERHEIJ

TABLE OF CONTENTS

Chapter 1
Introduction

Chapter 1
Introduction

Computers can be used to support tasks that involve argumentation. Computer programs that can support argumentative tasks are called *argument assistants*. Just as word-processing software assists the process of writing, e.g., by making it easy to move text from one place to another and by providing automatic spelling checks, argument assistance software assists with argumentative tasks. Argument assistants can, for instance, help with the organization, visualization and evaluation of arguments.

In this book, no attempt is made to cover all aspects of argumentation. The focus in this book is on *defeasible argumentation*, especially as it occurs in the law. In defeasible argumentation, it may occur that a conclusion that is at first sight justified by an argument, is later withdrawn, for instance because there are new reasons against the conclusion. Since in legal argumentation defeasibility is omnipresent and often crucial, the law is chosen as the domain of application.

More specifically, the focus is on the following four aspects of argumentation: arguing with pros and cons, arguing with warrants, argument evaluation, and theory construction. These aspects of argumentation are all common in the domain of law. The argument assistants discussed in this book provide assistance with these four aspects of argumentation.

After a general introduction to argument assistants (section 1.1), the defeasibility of argumentation in the field of law is discussed (section 1.2). This leads to a view of the application of the law to concrete cases in terms of theory construction (section 1.3). An important question is then how information technology, and especially artificial intelligence research, can deal with argumentation. The question is addressed in section 1.4, where argument assistance is distinguished from automated reasoning. In section 1.5, the experimental argument assistants presented in this book are introduced: ARGUE! and the systems in the ARGUMED family. In section 1.6, pointers are given to related research. The chapter concludes with a legal case that is used as an example throughout the book (section 1.7).

1.1 Argument Assistants

Argument assistants are computer programs that assist users with argumentative tasks. Argumentative tasks occur in many kinds of situations. For instance, people draft argumentative texts, try to justify points of view, take part in debates between opponents or in opinion forming discussions, they must make decisions, and try to choose rationally between several options.

A domain in which argumentation plays a dominant role is the law. The following observations exemplify the mentioned argumentative tasks in a legal setting:

- Lawyers routinely *produce argumentative texts*, such as court pleadings.
- A legal opinion is worth as much as the *justification* that is given to support it.
- In the courtroom, *debate between opponents* has been institutionalized.
- *Opinion formation* concerning matters of law is an important task of legal research.
- Judges are authoritative *decision makers*.
- Lawyers must try to *choose rationally* between different courses of action, for instance when giving advice to a client or determining whether or not to prosecute a suspect.

All these situations involve argumentation. There are issues to be settled, and for that purpose arguments are produced. These arguments are based on assumptions and contain reasons for and against the issues involved.

In these terms, argument assistance software can for instance help with argumentative tasks by

- keeping track of the issues that are raised and the assumptions that are made,
- keeping track of the reasons that have been adduced for and against a conclusion,
- keeping track of the issues that have been settled or remain open,
- providing means to organize the statements made,
- providing tools for argument evaluation,

- providing argument templates, and
- checking constraints that must be obeyed.

The research presented in this book originated in the interdisciplinary field of artificial intelligence and law. The law is of course a fruitful source of examples of argumentation. Moreover, many – if not all – of the most difficult questions with respect to argumentation occur within the law in a real-life context. As a result, many examples in the book will be taken from the legal domain. The general reader will however discover that most of what is said is relevant in a context which is wider than the law.

1.2 Defeasible Argumentation in the Field of Law

Argumentation is a vast topic. As a result, the software described in this book was developed with a restricted perspective on argumentation in mind. The selection of focal points has been made with an eye on legal reasoning. Especially, defeasibility of argumentation lies at the heart of the research in this book.

In all argumentation software to be discussed in this book, the argumentation involves statements that are not only supported by arguments for them, but they are also attacked by arguments against. In short, the focus is on *arguing with pros and cons*.

One natural context in which to study arguing with pros and cons, is that of dialogues in which two or more arguers exchange arguments for and against the statements made. For instance, it can be the case that in a particular dialogue two arguers have dedicated roles: one arguer tries to defend a claim by giving reasons for it, while another tries to raise doubts by providing reasons against the claim.

In the present book, argumentation is however not studied in a dialogue context. Instead, argumentation is treated as a process of finding satisfactory assumptions to settle one or more issues. In other words, argumentation is regarded as a kind of *theory construction*: the assumptions determined in the process of argumentation provide a theory to settle the issues.

For instance, a judge uses his knowledge of the law and of the world in general, the available evidence and the court proceedings in order to settle the issue as to whether a criminal suspect is innocent or guilty. It regularly occurs that the available information contains conflicting material (for instance, contradictory witness testimonies) and does not suffice to settle the issue. As a result, the judge will have to form an acceptable theory of the case. A first selection of reasonable hypotheses can for instance provide an initial theory with respect to the suspect's innocence. By subsequent critical scrutiny and adaptation of the theory, e.g., by arguing for and against its elements and consequences, the theory is developed until it provides a satisfactory account of the case and the suspect's innocence. The theory construction view on argumentation is especially relevant when it is acknowledged that argumentation is defeasible, since in that case the status of an issue can change throughout the process.

A topic requiring special attention when considering argumentation with pros and cons is *argument evaluation*. The standard view on argument evaluation is provided by classical logic in terms of logical validity (whether in a semantic, proof-theoretic or procedural guise). For instance, an argument is regarded as valid when the truth of its conclusion follows from the truth of its premises. This standard view requires adaptation, however, since arguing with pros and cons is defeasible: a conclusion that is justified given a particular set of arguments can cease to be justified when arguments are added. This can, for instance, occur when a reason against a conclusion is introduced. When there are only reasons for punishing someone, it seems to be justified to conclude that he must be punished. However, when sufficient counter-reasons become available it may occur that it is no longer justified to draw that conclusion. It can even happen that it is justified to draw the opposite conclusion, that he must not be punished.

The result of the defeasibility of argumentation with pros and cons is that a corresponding argument evaluation function cannot be monotonic. An argument evaluation function is monotonic when adding information can only extend the set of justified conclusions and never leads to a smaller set of justified conclusions. Since evaluation in terms of standard logical validity is monotonic, the notion of argument evaluation must be revised. The defeasibility of reasoning and the corresponding nonmonotonicity of consequence relations has received a great deal of research attention since the 1980s and has turned out to be a difficult and subtle subject.

A perspective on argumentation is not complete without a discussion of *warrants*, in the way that Toulmin (1958) used the term, viz., as generic inference licences. For Toulmin, warrants are rule-like statements warranting that some reason supports its conclusion. For instance, the statement that murderers should be imprisoned for twenty years can warrant the argument that a particular suspect should be imprisoned for twenty years since he is a murderer. Dealing with warrants is especially intricate in the context of defeasible argumentation, since it is often the case that warrants have exceptions. For instance, even when in general the warrant obtains that murderers should be imprisoned for twenty years, it can occur that a specific murderer should *not* be imprisoned, e.g., when he is considered to be mentally ill.

Especially in an account of legal argumentation, warrants cannot be missed. Many of the issues in legal reasoning concern the question whether a particular warrant is justified. This occurs for instance in a debate on the interpretation of a particular statutory article. From an argumentation-theoretic point of view, such a debate concerns settling the issue of which warrant (or warrants) are backed by the article.

Summarizing, the argumentation perspective in this book consists of four points of focus:

- Arguing with pros and cons
- Theory construction
- Argument evaluation
- Arguing with warrants

All four are of central relevance for defeasible argumentation in the law.

1.3 Theory Construction and the Application of Law to Cases

Theory construction provides a view on the application of law to cases. A somewhat naïve conception of the application of the law to concrete cases is that it consists of strictly following the given rules of law that match the given case facts – a conception by which a judge is turned into a *bouche de la loi* (Figure 1.1).

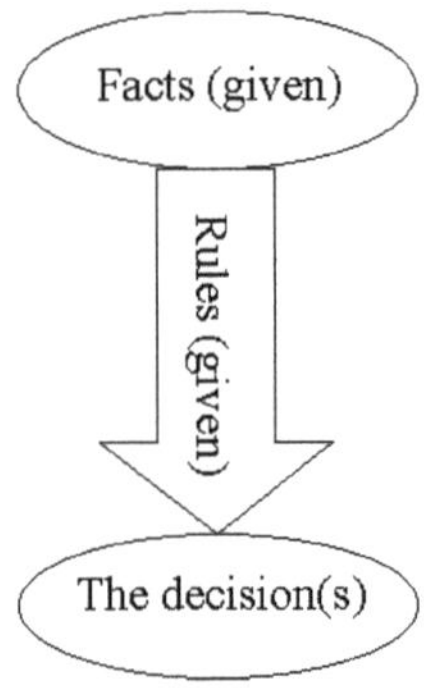

Figure 1.1: A naïve view of applying the law to a case

The main problem with this view (which has become a mock image of law application that mainly serves as a take-off point from which to move away) is that it assumes that the rules of law and the case facts are somehow readily available. Obviously, this is not the case. The available material is simply not sufficiently precise and unambiguous to allow the straightforward application of rules to facts. And even if the rules and facts were given in an adequate manner, following the rules that match the case facts can be problematic. First, following the rules may not be appropriate, e.g., when a rule is not applicable because of an exception. Second, it may be that the case is not solved at all, e.g., when no relevant result follows. Third, there may be several possibilities, perhaps ones which even conflict.

The first can occur since legal rules are generally *defeasible*. There can be exclusionary reasons or reasons against their application, for instance when applying the rule would be against its purpose.

The second is the case when there is a legal *gap*: the applicable law does not have an answer to the current case. This not only occurs on the advent of new legally relevant phenomena (such as the new legal problems as they are encountered by the rise of the internet), but also when the law only (and often deliberately) provides a partial answer, as for instance by the use of open rule conditions, such as grievous bodily harm or fairness. An adjudicator will have to fill the gap, for instance by making new rules of classification.

The third is the case when there is a legal *ambiguity*: the applicable law provides several possible answers. This can occur by accident, for instance, when there is an unforeseen and unwanted conflict of rules. In a complex, man-made system such as the law, this is to be expected. Ambiguities also arise on purpose, however, namely when choosing between the different possibilities is left to the discretion of the adjudicator. For instance, in the Netherlands, rules of criminal law have open rule conclusions, in the sense that they merely prescribe the maximum punishment. As a result, the adjudicator can take all circumstances into account when deciding the actual punishment to be imposed.

Defeasibility is related to the dialectics that are so deeply entrenched in the law: every claim can at times be subject to discussion. Legal gaps and ambiguities are signs of the inherent openness of the legal system. Just as defeasibility, they allow for a flexible application of the law that takes all circumstances into account, and they can thus increase the system's justness.[1]

In a view of applying the law to cases that is different from the naïve conception, law application is considered as a kind of dialectical theory construction (Figure 1.2; cf., also section 1.3). In such a view, applying the law to a case is a process which goes through a series of stages. During the process, a theory of the case, the applicable law and the consequences is progressively developed. The process starts with a preliminary theory with imperfections, such as insufficiently justified assumptions, tentative interpretations of legal sources, unduly applied rules, open issues and conflicting conclusions. During the process, the theory is gradually enhanced in order to diminish the imperfections. The process is guided by examining the preliminary theory, and by looking for reasons for and against it.

The argument assistants presented in the present book support the dialectical theory construction needed for the application of the law to cases.[2]

---

[1] Some may fear that defeasibility, gaps and ambiguities all too easily diminish legal security and equality. One asset of the legal system is that it tries to uphold legal security and equality by explicit specification, while leaving room for justness by remaining open.

[2] I first made the connection between theory construction and argument assistants in a paper on the theory of Crombag, Van Koppen and Wagenaar on anchored narratives (Verheij 2000b). The theory of anchored narratives focuses on the role of evidence in legal decision making (Crombag, Van Koppen and Wagenaar 1994, Wagenaar, Van Koppen and Crombag 1993).

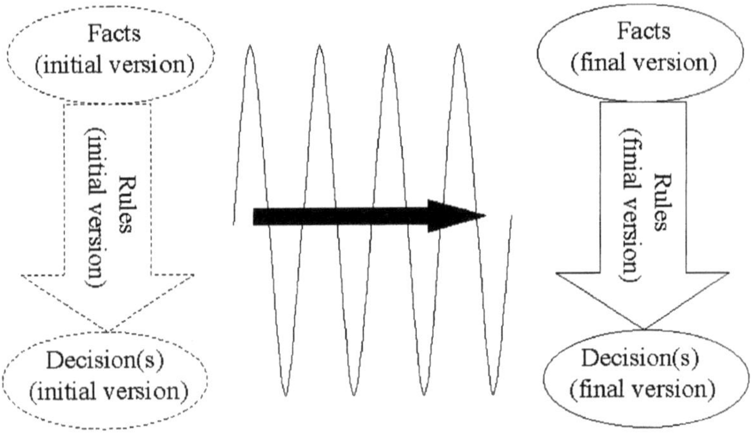

Figure 1.2: Theory construction

1.4 From Automated Reasoning to Argument Assistance: the Artificial Intelligence Perspective

The points of focus concerning argumentation discussed above (arguing with pros and cons, arguing with warrants, argument evaluation and theory construction) concern challenging aspects of argumentation, both in theory and in practice. Is it reasonable to expect that information technology, and in particular artificial intelligence, can deal with them? It is time to address the perspective of artificial intelligence.

The idea of building intelligent machines has been around for a long time. And since the start of the computer age in the 1940s, when the first computers (such as the famous ENIAC) were built, the progress has been impressive. Automated data processing, the personal computer, the Internet and mobile computing continue to have tremendous impact. Computers can defeat chess grandmasters. Machines can recognize handwritten text. Robots can learn to walk. Knowledge-based systems can improve the work of human experts in law and in medicine.

Not all expectations have been met, though. An infamous prediction is Herbert Simon's in 1957 that 'in a visible future' the range of problems that machines and human minds can handle would become coextensive (Russell and Norvig 1995, p. 20). He did not see this future: Simon died in 2001. In particular knowledge-intensive, underspecified tasks, such as language understanding and legal decision making, still pose extensive and difficult problems.

Considering these problems, it makes sense to combine the strengths of computers and humans. More concretely, it can be investigated how computer systems can support tasks performed by humans, instead of replacing them. In this book, this approach is taken with respect to argumentation. The design effort reported upon in this book was not aimed at the development of software that can reason autonomously and automatically, but of software that can support human reasoning. The former type of software is referred to as automated reasoning systems, the latter as argument assistance systems, or argument assistants, for short.[3]

Clearly, argument assistants must be distinguished from automated reasoning systems, which are more common. The latter automatically perform reasoning on the basis of the information in their 'knowledge base'. In this way, an automated reasoning system can carry out reasoning tasks for the user. Argument assistants do not (or do not primarily) reason autonomously; the goal of assistance systems is not to replace the user's reasoning, but to assist the user in his reasoning process.

The different nature of argument assistance systems and automated reasoning systems has two consequences. First, argument assistants are more reactive than active, in comparison with automated reasoning systems. Argument assistants provide a setting for performing argumentative tasks, set constraints and provide guidance. In an argument assistant, some functions can occur automatically 'in the background' instead of when a user gives a command. For instance, the evaluation of argumentative data, such as the indication which statements are currently justified, can be computed automatically, much like the spelling checks of word processing systems: after each action by the user, the argument assistance system updates previous evaluations.

Second, in the development of argument assistants, some of the difficulties of building automated reasoning systems can be avoided or become less critical. For instance, the acquisition and representation of knowledge become less of a bottleneck since such tasks can to a large extent be left to the user (or users) of an argument assistance system: using such a system

[3] See also Hunter's (2001) discussion of hybrid argumentation systems.

can in fact come down to constructing a representation of the arguments that are relevant to the problem at hand. A side-effect of the mediation of the construction by the argument assistant is that the representation becomes available in a format that is – at least partially – understandable to the system. Perhaps more importantly, the responsibility for the representation remains largely on the side of the user, and can be adapted at will.

In the law, the acquisition and representation of knowledge are especially notorious because of the law's inherent complexities, such as its open and dynamic nature. As a consequence, a computer representation of a part of the law can hardly ever be complete and will easily become obsolete. By leaving a considerable part of the representational tasks to the user, these complexities are less intense for argument assistance systems than for automated reasoning systems. In fact, this is a relevant incentive to develop argument assistants in the first place (cf., also Leenes 1998).

1.5 Experimental Argument Assistants: Argue! and the ArguMed Family

In the following chapters a series of computer programs for argument assistance will be discussed: Argue! and the ArguMed family. All can be downloaded at <www.rechten.unimaas.nl/metajuridica/verheij/aaa/>.

The first argument assistant, Argue! (chapter 2), was inspired by my work on the logical system CumulA that abstractly modelled defeasible argumentation (Verheij 1996a). In CumulA, arguments (in the sense of trees of reasons and conclusions) can be defeated. The defeat of arguments results from attack by other arguments, as expressed by defeaters. A defeater indicates which set of arguments attacks which other set of arguments. CumulA's defeaters allow the representation of several types of defeat (including defeat by parallel strengthening and by sequential weakening; Verheij 1996a). While building Argue!, it became apparent, however, that CumulA (or rather: the streamlined version thereof used for Argue!) was not sufficiently natural for the representation of real-life argumentation. Also the on-screen drawing of argumentative data (especially of the defeaters) seemed to be too complex for the intended users. The result was a system that was mainly interesting from a research perspective, as a realization of (and a testbed for) a particular theory of defeasible argumentation. Argue! was first described in this way by Verheij (1998a).

After the development of the ARGUE! system, a new approach was taken, resulting in the systems of the ARGUMED family. There were two starting points. First, the argumentation theory was changed considerably. The focus was on the statements and reasons that occur in argumentation, instead of on the arguments. Second, the interface became template-based. The user could perform his argumentation by filling in forms dedicated to particular argument moves.

With respect to the argumentation theory, the focus was limited to undercutting exceptions, as distinguished by Pollock (1987, 1995): reasons that block the connection between a reason and a conclusion. Since undercutting exceptions are of established importance for legal reasoning (see, e.g., Prakken 1997, Hage 1997, Verheij 1996a), this seemed to be a natural choice. The first version of ARGUMED (ARGUMED 1.0; Verheij 1998b, not further discussed in the present book) was soon replaced by the second since it had two obvious drawbacks: undercutting exceptions were not represented graphically, and it was not possible to argue about certain relevant issues, such as whether a statement was a reason or not, or whether it was an exception or not. The former drawback was solved in ARGUMED 2.0 (chapter 3) by the use of dialectical arguments, in which support by reasons and attack by undercutting exceptions were represented simultaneously. The latter led to the introduction of step and undercutter warrants. In ARGUMED 2.0, a step warrant is a kind of conditional sentence that underlies an argument step, such as 'If Peter has violated a property right, then he has committed a tort'. Undercutter warrants similarly underlie attack by an undercutting exception. An example of an undercutter warrant is the statement 'The statement that there is a ground of justification for Peter's act, is an exception to the rule that, if Peter has violated a property right, then Peter has committed a tort'. Verheij (1999a) gave the first presentation of ARGUMED 2.0.

A qualitative user evaluation of ARGUMED 2.0 involving ten test persons (see section 3.4) inspired the design of a new user interface of the system. The result was ARGUMED 3.0 (chapter 4). Its user interface is based on a mouse-sensitive argument screen, in accordance with what the test persons had expected. When the user double-clicks in the argument screen, a box appears in which a statement can be typed. The right mouse button gives access to a context-sensitive menu that allows adding support for or attack against a statement. The resulting interface is very natural and easy to use, as was confirmed by another user evaluation (see section 4.4). Apart from the better interface, the most interesting enhancement of the new version of ArguMed is that it uses a richer and more satisfactory argumentation theory. Whereas in ArguMed 2.0 the only kind of attack was based on undercutting exceptions, ArguMed 3.0 allows the attack of any statement. By considering the connecting arrows between statements (whether expressing support or attack) as conditional statements, warrants and undercutters found natural representations. Moreover, the new version of ArguMed is logically more satisfactory: the evaluation of dialectical arguments corresponds exactly to the dialectical interpretations of prima facie justified assumptions in the logical system DefLog (see Verheij 2000a, 2003).

The main part of the book consists of descriptions of the systems and their argumentation theories (chapters 2, 3 and 4). In order to illustrate the possibilities and differences, one example is used throughout the discussion of the three systems. This example is discussed in section 1.7 below.

1.6 Related Research

The research reported on in this book is connected with previous work on various topics. Among the most relevant related research is that on argument assistants and argument mediators. A selection of that work is discussed in chapter 5. Also the abundance of work on defeasible argumentation has been an inspiration (see chapter 6). Other relevant topics that have been investigated in recent research are for instance the following:

- Dialogical theories of reasoning. Hage (2000) provides an insightful overview. See for instance Gordon's (1995) Pleadings Game and Lodder's (1998) DiaLaw. Both focus on the field of law.
- Computer-supported argumentation in teaching and learning. See for instance Aleven's (1997) work on CATO, related to Ashley's (1990) HYPO, Bench-Capon and Leng (1998), and – not focusing on the legal domain – Suthers et al. (1995) on Belvedere, Veerman (2000), Van Gelder (2001).
- Argument analysis. For instance, Reed and Walton (2001) are developing Araucaria, see <www.computing.dundee.ac.uk/staff/creed/

research/araucaria.html>. They build on Walton's work on argumentation schemes (Walton 1996). See also Verheij (2001b).
- Computer-supported collaborative work focusing on argumentation. See Shum's web site at <kmi.open.ac.uk/people/sbs/csca/>.
- Computer-supported and online legal mediation and dispute resolution (see, e.g., Lodder and Huygen 2001, <www.mediate.com and www.odrworkshop.org>).
- Discourse systems focusing on e-democracy and e-governance applications. See especially Gordon's web site at <www.tfgordon.de>.
- Knowledge management. Cf., e.g., Stranieri and Zeleznikow (2000).
- Case management and litigation support systems. See, e.g., <www.digital-lawyer.com/digital-lawyer/resource/caseman.html>.
- Reasoning with evidence in the law. Cf., Wagenaar, Van Koppen and Crombag (1993), Crombag, Van Koppen and Wagenaar (1994), MacCrimmon and Tillers (2002), Verheij (2000b), Prakken, Reed and Walton (2003).
- Epistemology. Cf., e.g., Pollock (1986, 1995). Especially relevant is legal epistemology. Cf., e.g., Peczenik (1989), Brouwer (1990), Ruiter (1993), Peczenik and Hage (2000), Mommers (2002).
- Legal logic. Cf., e.g., Soeteman (1989), Hage (1997), Prakken (1997), Verheij (1999b), Verheij, Hage and Van Maanen (1999), Hage (2001b).

The present book focuses on argument assistants that have been developed with a legal context in mind, and in which the argumentation is defeasible.

1.7 An Example: A Case of Grievous Bodily Harm

Consider the following fictitious case of grievous bodily harm:

> 'There has been a pub fight, in which someone is badly injured: according to the hospital report, the victim has several broken ribs, with complications. Someone is arrested and accused of intentionally inflicting grievous bodily harm, which is punishable by up to eight years imprisonment, according to Article 302 Dutch criminal code [*wetboek van strafrecht*]. The accused denies that he was involved in the fight. However, there are ten witnesses who claim

> that the accused was involved. In one precedent (referred to as precedent 1), the victim has several broken ribs, but no complications. In that precedent, the bodily harm was not considered to be grievous, and the accused was punished for intentionally inflicting ordinary bodily harm, which is punishable with up to two years of imprisonment (Art. 300 Dutch criminal code). In another precedent (referred to as precedent 2), the victim has several broken ribs with complications. In precedent 2, the accused was punished for intentionally inflicting grievous bodily harm'.

The facts of the case can give rise to interesting argumentation concerning the accused's punishability for inflicting grievous bodily harm. In the discussion of the three systems, it will be shown to what extent the relevant argumentation can be produced within each of them.

Chapter 2
The First Prototype: ARGUE!

Chapter 2
The First Prototype: ARGUE!

The ARGUE! system is the first experimental argument assistant that will be discussed. After a treatment of its argumentation theory (section 2.1), the grievous bodily harm example of section 1.7 is used as an illustration (section 2.2). The chapter ends with a discussion of the ARGUE!'s program design (section 2.3).

2.1 ARGUMENTATION THEORY

The argumentation theory underlying the ARGUE! system was inspired by CUMULA (Verheij 1996a). CUMULA is a procedural model of argumentation with arguments and counterarguments. It is based on two main assumptions. The first assumption is that argumentation is a *process* during which arguments are constructed and counterarguments are adduced. The second assumption is that the arguments used in argumentation are *defeasible*, in the sense that whether they justify their conclusion depends on the counterarguments available at a stage of the argumentation process. If an argument no longer justifies its conclusion it is said to be defeated. The defeat of an argument is caused by a counterargument (that is itself undefeated).

For instance, if a colleague entering the room is completely soaked and states that it is raining outside, one could conclude that it is necessary to put on a raincoat. The conclusion can be rationally justified, by providing support for such a conclusion. For example, the following argument could be given:

> A colleague entering the room is completely soaked and states that it is raining.
> So, it is probably raining.
> So, it is necessary to put on a raincoat.

Such an argument is a reconstruction of how a conclusion can be supported.

An argument that supports its conclusion does not always justify it. For instance, if in our example it turns out that the streets are wet, but the sky is blue, the conclusion that it is necessary to put on a raincoat would no longer be justified. The argument has become *defeated.* For instance, the following argument could be given:

> The streets are wet, but the sky is blue.
> So, the shower is over.

In this case the argument that it is probably raining is defeated by the *counterargument* that the shower is over. Since the conclusion that it is probably raining is no longer justified, it can no longer support the conclusion that it is necessary to put on a raincoat.

CUMULA is a procedural model of argumentation with arguments and counterarguments, in which the defeat status of an argument, either undefeated or defeated, depends on three factors:

(1) the structure of the argument;
(2) the attacks by counterarguments;
(3) the argumentation stage.

We will briefly discuss each factor below. The model continues the work of Pollock (1987, 1995), Simari and Loui (1992), Vreeswijk (1993, 1997) and Dung (1995) in philosophy and artificial intelligence, and was developed to complement the work on the model of rules and reasons, Reason-Based Logic (see, e.g., Hage 1996, 1997 and Verheij 1996a).

In CUMULA, the structure of an argument (factor (1) above) is represented as in the argumentation theory of Van Eemeren and Grootendorst (1981, 1987). Both the subordination and the coordination of arguments are possible. It is explored how the structure of arguments can lead to their defeat. For instance, the intuitions that it is easier to defeat an argument if it contains a longer chain of defeasible steps ('sequential weakening'), and that it is more difficult to defeat an argument if it contains more reasons to support its conclusion ('parallel strengthening'), are investigated.

In the CUMULA model, which arguments are counterarguments for other arguments, i.e., which arguments can *attack* other arguments (factor (2) above), is taken as the primitive notion (cf., Dung 1995). This approach to argument defeat can be called *counterargument-triggered defeat*. Basically, an argument is defeated if it is attacked by an undefeated counterargument. This approach to argument defeat must be contrasted with *inconsistency-triggered defeat*, where the primitive notion is which arguments have conflicting conclusions (as, e.g., in Vreeswijk's 1993, 1997 abstract argumentation systems). In this approach to argument defeat, an argument is defeated if there is an undefeated argument with a conflicting conclusion. Often the defeating argument has higher priority than the defeated argument, with respect to some priority relation on arguments.[1]

In CUMULA, so-called *defeaters* indicate which arguments are counterarguments to other arguments, i.e., which arguments can defeat other arguments. In this way, CUMULA shows that the defeasibility of arguments can be fully modelled in terms of argument structure and the attack relation between arguments, independent of the underlying language. Moreover, it turns out that defeaters can be used to represent a wide range of types of defeat, as proposed in the literature, e.g., Pollock's (1987) undercutting and rebutting defeat. Also some new types of defeat can be distinguished, namely defeat by sequential weakening (related to the well-known sorites paradox) and defeat by parallel strengthening (related to the accrual of reasons).

In the CUMULA model, argumentation stages (factor (3) above) represent the arguments and the counterarguments currently taken into account, and the status of these arguments, either defeated or undefeated. The model's lines of argumentation, i.e., sequences of stages, provide insight into the way in which the status of arguments is affected by the arguments taken into account in the course of the process. For instance, by means of argumentation diagrams (which provide an overview of the possible lines of argumentation), phenomena that are characteristic for argumentation with defeasible arguments, such as the reinstatement of arguments, are explicitly depicted. In contrast to Vreeswijk's (1993, 1997) model, it is shown how in a line of argumentation not only new conclusions are inferred ('forward argumentation', or inference), but also new reasons are adduced ('backward argumentation', or justification). In other words, CUMULA's model of

[1] I made the distinction between counterargument-triggered and inconsistency-triggered defeat in my dissertation (Verheij 1996a). I think that (Dung-style) counterargument-triggered defeat is philosophically the most attractive and innovative of the two approaches to argument defeat.

the argumentation process is free, as opposed to premise-based systems (that focus on inference from a fixed set of premises) and issue-based systems (that focus on justification of a fixed set of issues): in CumulA neither the premises nor the issues are fixed during a line of argumentation.

To summarize, CumulA shows

(1) how the subordination and coordination of arguments is related to argument defeat;
(2) how the defeat of arguments can be described in terms of their structure, counterarguments, and the stage of the argumentation process, and independent of the logical language;
(3) how both inference and justification can be formalized in one model.

CumulA has obvious limitations. We can mention two. First, its underlying language is completely unstructured. It contains, for instance, no logical connectives, no quantifiers, and no modal operators. This is certainly a limitation, but one of the research objectives was to show that defeat can be fruitfully studied independently of the language. Second, the role of the rules underlying arguments is not clarified in CumulA. This is in part due to the first limitation: the language of CumulA does not contain a conditional or variables, by which rules would become expressible.[2]

Verheij (1996a) discusses the CumulA model extensively, both informally and formally.

2.2 The Grievous Bodily Harm Example

As an illustration, it is shown how argumentation concerning the grievous bodily harm example (section 1.7) can be represented in Argue!.

To begin with, an argument is constructed for the conclusion that the accused is punishable by up to 8 years imprisonment (figure 2.1). This is done by typing statements in on-screen boxes and connecting the state-

[2] Verheij (1996a) discusses a formal model in which rules play a central role, viz., Reason-Based Logic. However, the formal connection with the CumulA model is not made. The reason for this is, among other things, the very different 'flavours' of the two formalisms.

ments by drawing arrows. Here the conclusions are drawn above the reasons for them, but the user can arrange the statements at will.

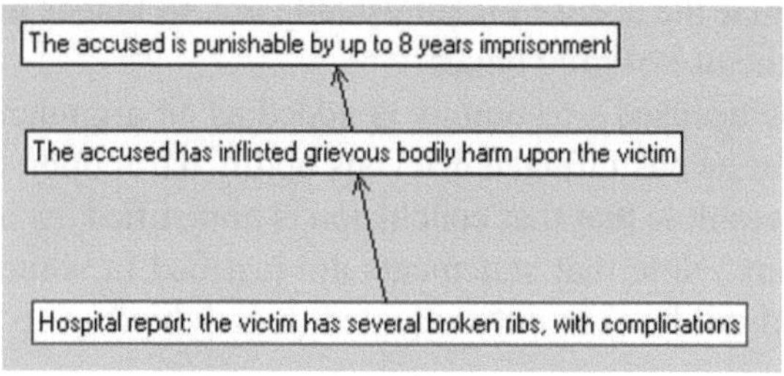

Figure 2.1: A two-step argument

In figure 2.1, all three statements are justified, as is indicated by the use of white boxes. The hospital report statement is set as justified (by the user, as is indicated by a box with a different colour edge), the other two are justified since there is a justifying reason for each of them.

Next, precedent 1 is used to argue that broken ribs do not amount to 'grievous' bodily harm. The user adds the appropriate statements, and draws the dedicated graphical structure that represents a defeater (figure 2.2). Here the rule that several broken ribs do not amount to grievous bodily harm, which explains the precedent, is used as a counterargument against the connection between the hospital report statement and the conclusion that grievous bodily harm has been inflicted. This is an example of an undercutting defeater (cf., Pollock 1987).

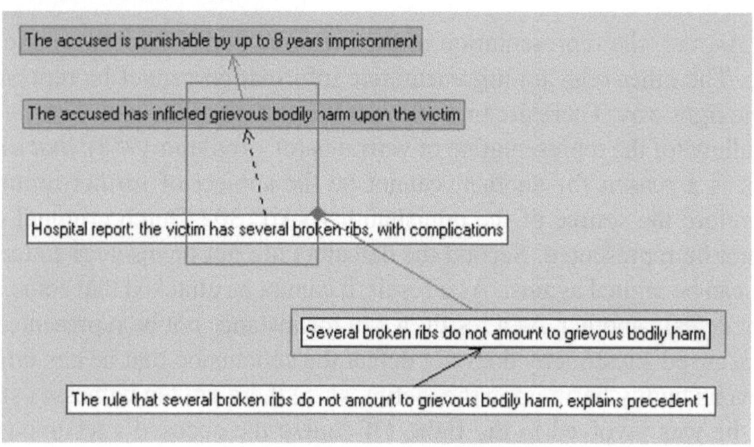

Figure 2.2: Adding a defeater

The result is that the connecting arrow is no longer supporting (indicated by the dots). Therefore the conclusions that grievous bodily harm has been inflicted and that the accused is punishable are no longer justified. This is indicated by the use of grey boxes.

Finally, the accused's testimony is added as an argument attacking the conclusion that he has inflicted grievous bodily harm upon the victim (figure 2.3). The result is that that conclusion is unjustified, as indicated by the crossed-out box. Note that statements are justified (a white box), unjustified (a crossed-out box) or not evaluated (a grey box).

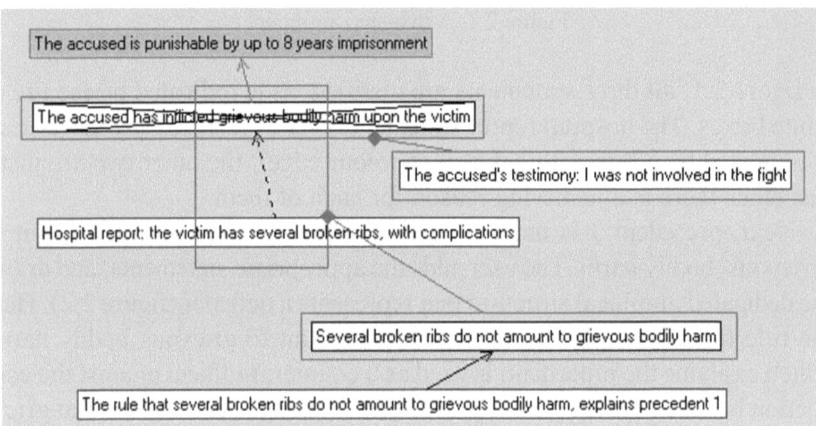

Figure 2.3: A second defeater

For ARGUE!, the representation of the grievous bodily harm example ends here. The other relevant argumentative information cannot be represented in the right way. There are two relevant limitations of ARGUE!. First, it does not allow for the representation of warrants (cf., Toulmin 1958): *that* a statement is a reason for another, cannot be the subject of further argument. Therefore the source of the punishability (Art. 302 Dutch criminal code) cannot be represented. Second the defeaters are not themselves statements that can be argued against. As a result, it cannot be attacked that some argument defeats another. As a result, it can for instance not be represented that the accused's testimony does not defeat the conclusion that he has inflicted grievous bodily harm upon the victim, since there are ten witnesses stating that he was involved in the fight. Of course the accused's testimony can itself be argued against, but that would be a misrepresentation of the example: there is no reason to dispute the accused's testimony, only its defeating effect is at issue.

2.3 PROGRAM DESIGN

ARGUE!'s opening screen is shown in figure 2.4.

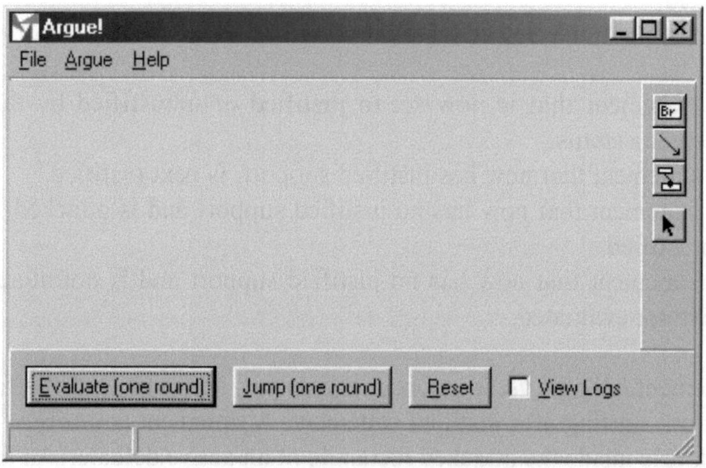

Figure 2.4: ARGUE!'s opening screen

In the ARGUE! system, the user 'draws' his argumentation on screen. By clicking one of the buttons on the left, the user chooses the graphical mode. There are four modes, viz., statement mode, arrow mode, defeater mode and selection mode. In statement mode, clicking in the drawing area shows an edit box, in which a sentence can be typed. In arrow mode, statements can be connected by arrows, indicating that a statement is a reason for another. In order to draw an arrow, the user clicks twice: first on the reason statement, second on the conclusion statement. In defeater mode, defeaters are drawn. They consist of two connected rectangles. In order to draw a defeater, the user makes two selections in the drawing area (by clicking and dragging). The first selection indicates the attacking part of the argumentative data, the second the attacked part. Only the statements and arrows that are selected are attacking or attacked, not the defeaters. In selection mode, the user can select argumentative elements in the drawing area. For instance, a statement can be moved by clicking and dragging. Statements and arrows can be deleted.

ARGUE! has a step by step evaluation algorithm, activated by clicking the 'Evaluate (one round)' button. At each step, the current statuses of the argumentative data determine the new statuses. The basis of the evaluation is formed by the statement statuses that are set by the user. By right-clicking a statement, the user can set a statement as justified, unjustified or not evaluated.

The evaluation rules are as follows:

1. A statement that is now set to justified or unjustified by the user, keeps its status.
2. A statement that now has justified support, is next justified.
3. A statement that now has no justified support and is attacked, is next unjustified.
4. A statement that now has no justified support and is not attacked, is next not evaluated.

A statement *has justified support* if, and only if, it is at the end of a supporting arrow starting at a justified statement. A statement *is attacked* if, and only if, it is inside the attacked rectangle of an active defeater. An arrow *is supporting* if, and only if, it is not inside the attacked rectangle of an active defeater. A defeater *is active* if, and only if, the statements in its attacking rectangle are justified and the arrows in its attacking rectangle are supporting.

The 'Jump (one round)' button activates a variant of the evaluation algorithm, in which a statement that now has no justified support and is not attacked, is next justified (instead of not evaluated). This rule has the effect that all statements are prima facie justified. The user can optionally change the selection of rules that are used when clicking either of the two buttons.

The changes of evaluation statuses are logged. It depends on the argumentative data whether new evaluations are made. Two configurations that do not lead to new evaluations (when using the 'Jump' rules) are shown in the figures 2.5 and 2.6.

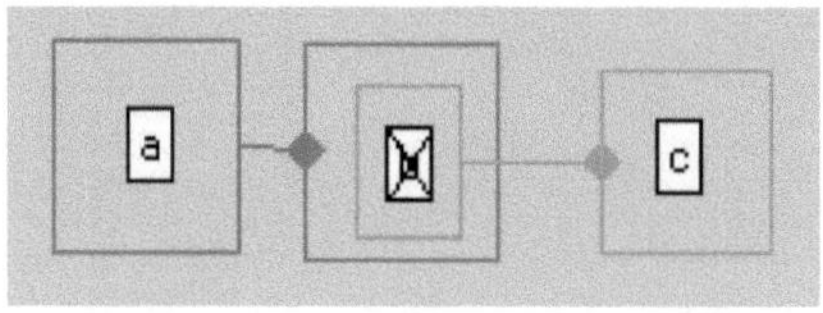

Figure 2.5: An attacking statement that is attacked by another statement

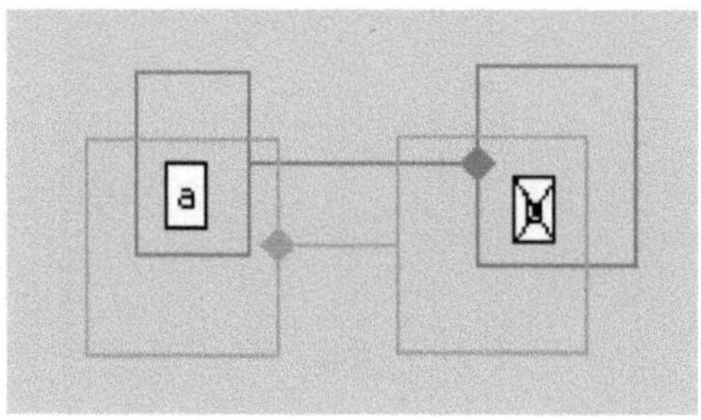

Figure 2.6: Two statements attacking each other

However, when in the second configuration, the statement 'a' is set to 'not evaluated', repeatedly clicking the 'Jump' button results in a loop flipping between two states: one in which both 'a' and 'b' are justified, and one in which both are unjustified. Further details are provided by Verheij (1998a).

Chapter 3
Improved Naturalness: ArguMed 2.0

Chapter 3
Improved Naturalness: ArguMed 2.0

The development of Argue! was soon followed by a series of argument assistants with starting points that differ fundamentally from those of Argue!: the ArguMed family. With respect to the program design, the starting point became that the argumentative data should be entered into the system by making argument moves instead of by drawing graphical elements. With respect to the argumentation theory, the starting point became that arguments are inherently dialectical, in the sense that support and attack go side by side and are not separated in different levels. The first member of the ArguMed family that will be discussed is ArguMed 2.0.[1]

3.1 Argumentation Theory

3.1.1 **Reasons, conclusions, exceptions**

The simplest form of an argument (in ArguMed's argumentation theory) is a statement, e.g.:

> Peter has committed a tort.

In an argument, reasons can be given for other statements, e.g.:

> Peter has committed a tort, since he has violated a property right.

In defeasible argumentation, it can be the case that a conclusion is not justified although there is a prima facie justifying reason for it. For instance, an undercutting exception (cf., Pollock's 1987 undercutting defeaters) can break the connection between a reason and a conclusion:

[1] Verheij (1998b) describes ArguMed 1.0.

> Peter has violated a property right. As a result, at first sight, he has committed a tort. However, there is a ground of justification for Peter's act. As a result, on second thoughts, Peter's violation of a property right does not justify that he has committed a tort.

It is characteristic of an undercutting exception that the prima facie conclusion is not replaced by its opposite, viz., that Peter has *not* committed a tort: there could be *another* reason justifying the conclusion that Peter has committed a tort, even though the reason that Peter has violated a property right, does not justify that conclusion.

Figure 3.1: A dialectical argument (without warrants)

In figure 3.1, the reason/conclusion/exception structure of an argument is graphically depicted. In the argument there are two reasons for the statement that Peter has committed a tort, viz., that he has violated a property right, and that he has acted against proper social conduct. Only the first of these reasons is blocked by an exception, viz., that there is a ground of justification.

Reason/conclusion/exception-structures, as depicted in figure 3.1, are (unwarranted) *dialectical arguments*. They can be thought of as structures of *argument steps*, i.e., the directed connections of reasons with their conclusions, and *argument undercutters*, i.e., steps with exceptions breaking the connection between the steps' reason and conclusion. The argument in figure 3.1 consists of three steps, and one undercutter that encompasses one of the steps. A reason for a conclusion can itself be supported by a reason (*subordination*), a conclusion can be supported by more than one reason (*coordination*), a step can be undercut by more than one exception (*multiple attack*), and reasons for undercutters can themselves be undercut (*counterattack*).

3.1.2 Warrants

It is not the case that *any* statement is a reason for *any* other statement. If a connection between a reason and a conclusion exists, the argument step from the reason to the conclusion is said to be *warranted*. That a certain statement implies another statement, in the sense that it can be adduced as a reason for the statement, is itself a statement, and can be expressed as follows:

If Peter has violated a property right, then he has committed a tort.

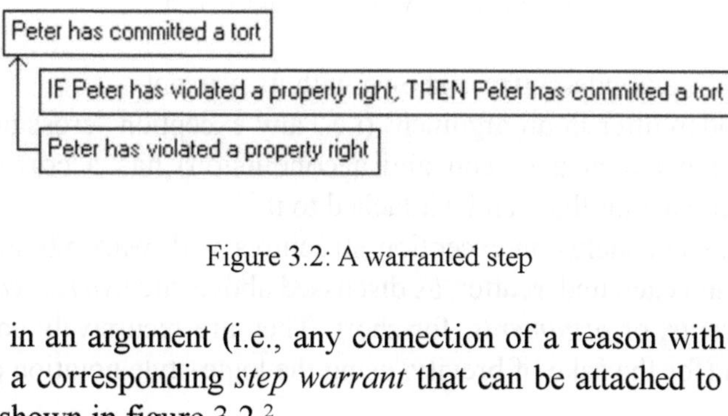

Figure 3.2: A warranted step

Any step in an argument (i.e., any connection of a reason with a conclusion) has a corresponding *step warrant* that can be attached to it. An example is shown in figure 3.2.[2]

Step warrants play a role that is analogous to that of the material implication in the classical rule of inference *Modus ponens* (from P and $P \rightarrow Q$, infer Q).

Analogously, it is not the case that *any* statement is an exception, breaking the connection between *any* reason and conclusion. Just as steps, undercutters need to be warranted. *That* some statement is an undercutting exception, is itself a statement. Such 'excepting statements' provide the warrants of undercutters. An *undercutter warrant* can be expressed as follows:

[2] The use of uppercase characters in the 'step warrant statement' in the figure are meant to suggest that IF ..., THEN ... should be considered as a two-place logical connective. A more 'logical' notation expressing a step warrant would, e.g., be $p \rightsquigarrow q$.

The statement that there is a ground of justification for Peter's act, is an exception to the rule that, if Peter has violated a property right, then Peter has committed a tort.

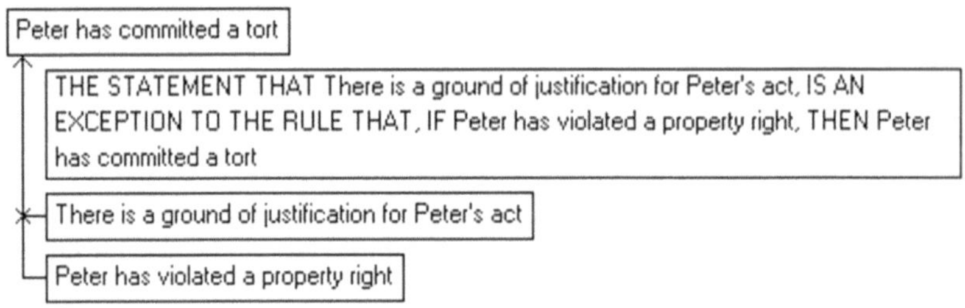

Figure 3.3: A warranted undercutter

In figure 3.3, an undercutter is shown with its warrant.

Any undercutter in an argument (i.e., any exception 'crossing out' the connection between a reason and a conclusion) has a corresponding undercutter warrant that can be attached to it.[3]

The reason/conclusion/exception structures with warrants attached to each step and each undercutter, as discussed above, are *warranted dialectical arguments*, or *arguments*, for short. They are recursively constructed as follows (for the sake of brevity, using the logic-style notation of notes 2 and 3):

1. A statement is an argument (containing one statement, no steps and no undercutters). Its conclusion and only premise are the statement itself.
2. Any argument containing a statement ψ can be extended with a step by adding statements $\varphi \rightsquigarrow \psi$ and φ to the argument. In the resulting argument, φ is a reason for ψ. The resulting argument's conclusion is that of the original argument; its premises are $\varphi \rightsquigarrow \psi$, φ and those of the original argument, minus φ.
3. Any argument containing a step consisting of $\varphi \rightsquigarrow \psi$ and φ can be extended with an undercutter by adding statements $\chi \rtimes (\varphi \rightsquigarrow \psi)$ and χ

[3] Sentences expressing undercutter warrants are obtained by a combination of other sentences, using the three-place logical connective THE STATEMENT THAT ..., IS AN EXCEPTION TO THE RULE THAT, IF ..., THEN ... . A more 'logical' notation expressing an undercutter warrant would, e.g., be $e \rtimes (p \rightsquigarrow q)$. Cf., note 2.

(for some χ) to the argument. In the resulting argument, χ is an exception to the step consisting of $\varphi \rightsquigarrow \psi$ and φ. The resulting argument's conclusion is that of the original argument; its premises are $\chi \rtimes (\varphi \rightsquigarrow \psi)$, χ and those of the original argument.

There can be more than one reason for a conclusion and more than one exception to a step.[4]

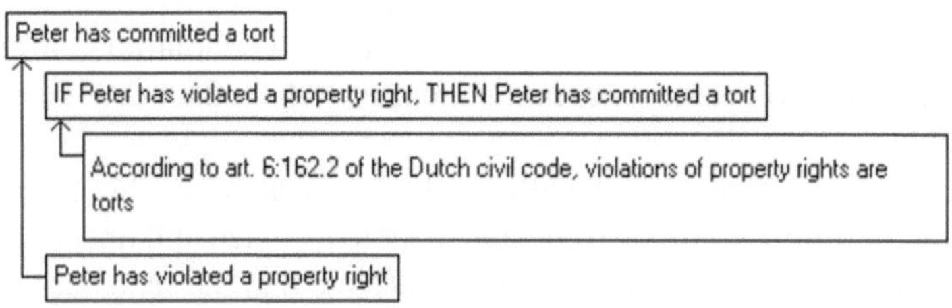

Figure 3.4: A reason for a step warrant

It may be thought that step warrants and undercutter warrants add little to an argument, and only make explicit what is already in the example steps and undercutters themselves. However, warrants can themselves be the *subject* of argumentation. An example is shown in figure 3.4. In this argument, a *reason* is adduced for the step warrant that, if Peter has violated a property right, then he has committed a tort. This reason is that, according to Article 6:162.2 Dutch civil code [*burgerlijk wetboek*], violations of property rights are torts.

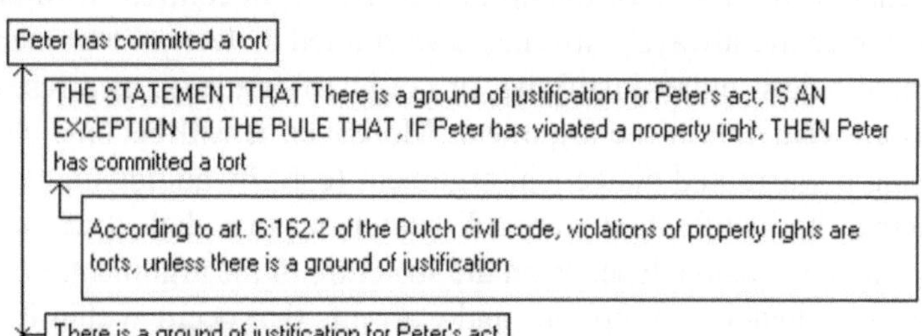

Figure 3.5: A reason for an undercutter warrant

[4] For now, the arguments are assumed to be finite. This holds true whenever there are no support or attack loops. See section 3.3.3.

Similarly, the argument in figure 3.5 shows an argument containing support for an undercutter warrant. In the example, the legal source of the exception (viz., Art. 6:162.2 Dutch civil code) is used to support that a ground of justification is an exception to the rule that violations of property rights are torts.

Note that in the arguments shown in figures 3.4 and 3.5 not all warrants are made explicit. For instance, in the argument of figure 3.4, there is a step without its corresponding warrant: the warrant of the step from the reason that, according to Article 6:162.2 Dutch civil code, violations of property rights are torts, to the step-warrant statement ('If ..., then ...'), is not made explicit.

Any dialectical argument with implicit warrants can be extended by attaching the appropriate warrant statement to any step and undercutter that does not yet have a warrant attached to it. (Note that the sentences expressing step warrants and undercutter warrants are the result of a formal combination of other sentences by an appropriate logical connective. Cf., notes 2 and 3.) In practice, it is convenient to leave implicit all warrants that are not themselves the subject of further argumentation.

3.1.3 **Justification**

Warranted dialectical arguments are the analogue for defeasible argumentation of the proofs of classical logic: a warranted dialectical argument demonstrates whether its conclusion is justified assuming its premises (i.e., the statements at the 'roots' of the argument 'tree'). In contrast with classical proofs, which are always justifying, a warranted dialectical argument is, as explicated below, either justifying, or not justifying, e.g., as a result of an exception occurring in the argument. Moreover, it will become clear that extending a warranted dialectical argument (e.g., by adding an exception) can change its justification status. Whether or not a dialectical argument justifies its conclusion depends on the structure of the argument, i.e., on the reasons, conclusions, exceptions and warrants that occur within it, and on the way they are related.

The justification status of an argument is here made dependent on given *assumptions* that do not necessarily include the premises of the argument. This allows arguments to have 'hanging' premises, i.e., premises that are not assumed, but that are, instead, an issue for further argumentation, which is convenient in practical argumentation (see below).

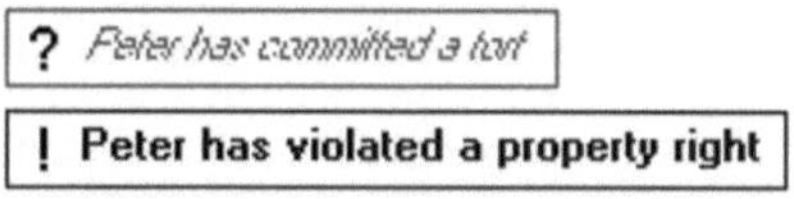

Figure 3.6: An issue and an assumption

For dialectical arguments with the simplest structure, viz., statements, the justification status with respect to the given assumptions is determined by the statement's type.[5] If the statement is itself an assumption, the justification status of the statement (considered as an argument with a trivial structure) is justifying. The 'conclusion' of the argument, i.e., the statement itself, is justified. If the statement is not an assumption – in which case it is called an *issue* – the statement is (as an argument) not justifying and (as a statement) not justified. In the figures, assumptions are marked with an exclamation mark, issues with a question mark. Statements that are justified are shown in a bold font, statements that are not justified are set in italic. For instance, in figure 3.6, the statement that Peter has committed a tort is an issue, while the statement that he has violated a property right is an assumption.

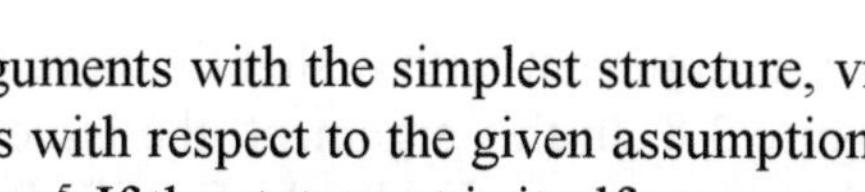

Figure 3.7: An issue justified by a justified reason

In an argument with no exceptions and no explicit step warrants, an issue is justified if there is a justified reason for it. For instance, the dialectical argument shown in figure 3.7 is justifying, and the issue that Peter has committed a tort is justified. Note that the example shows that – in the present use of terminology – issues need not be open, but can be settled. Here the issue is settled as justified. (Of course additional argumentation can turn a settled issue into an open issue and vice versa. See below.)

[5] As will be explained in chapter 4, this is not the case in ARGUMED 3.0, in which assumptions are prima facie justified, and can actually be defeated.

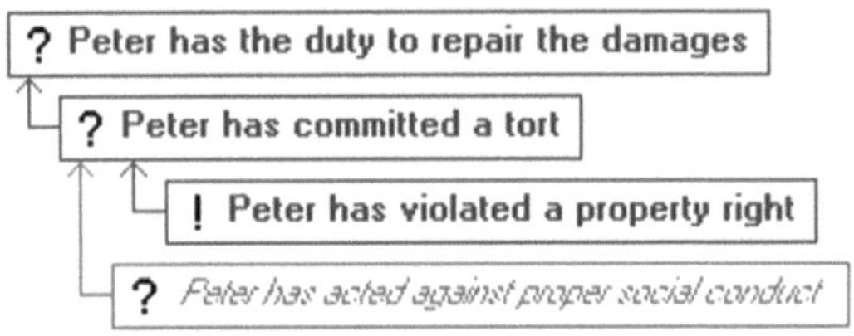

Figure 3.8: A hanging premise

A justifying dialectical argument with a slightly more complicated structure is shown in figure 3.8. In this argument, the issue that Peter has the duty to repair the damages, is justified by the (justified) reason that he has committed a tort. The issue that Peter has committed a tort, is also justified. There are two reasons that could justify it: that Peter has violated a property right and that he has acted against proper social conduct. Only the former justifies that Peter has committed a tort since it is a justified assumption. The latter reason (viz., that Peter has acted against proper social conduct) does not justify that Peter has committed a tort since it is an issue that is not justified (indicated by the italics). The issue is not justified since there is no reason justifying it.

The issue that Peter has acted against proper social conduct is an example of a *hanging premise* in an argument: a premise of an argument that is not assumed, but an issue for further argumentation. Hanging premises do not affect the justification status of the argument. As a result, in the present use of terminology premises and assumptions are very different notions. Briefly, the difference is as follows. Whether a statement is a premise is determined by the structure of the argument. Basically, a premise is one of the roots of an argument, i.e., the statements for which no reasons are adduced. In contrast, any statement – not only the argument's roots – can be assumptions since all statements have a type, either the assumption type or the issue type. Figure 3.9 contains an abstract example of the difference between assumptions and premises.

In the figure, a supports b, b supports c, c supports d and d supports e. Of the statements a, b, c, d and e only c is of the assumption type. The four others are issues. The statements c, d and e are justified, the statements a and b are not. The statement c is justified since it is an assumption. Although the statements d and e are issues, they are justified since there are justifying reasons for them, viz., c and d respectively. The statements a and

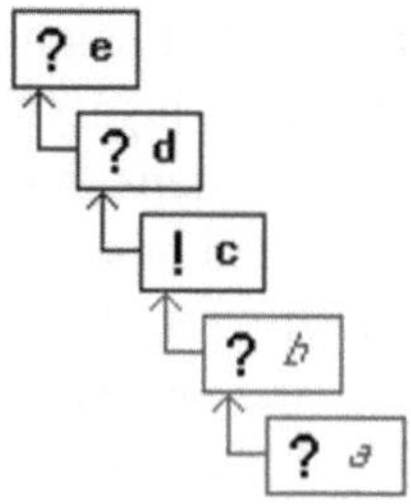

Figure 3.9: Assumptions and premises

b are not justified since they are issues for which there is no justifying reason. The statement a is a premise of the argument, but a hanging premise since it is an issue.

Of course, in the dynamic practice of argumentation, a hanging premise can become justified by a newly added reason. It is then no longer a root of the argument and therefore ceases to be a premise.

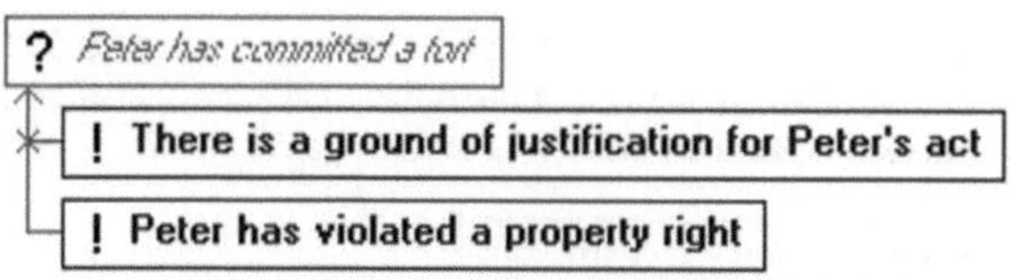

Figure 3.10: An exception making a reason non-justifying

Exceptions have the effect that a reason does not justify its conclusion, even if it is itself justified. For instance, the argument in figure 3.10 is not justifying, since the only reason for its conclusion is undercut by the exception that there is a ground of justification for Peter's act. The exception itself is trivially justified since it is an assumption.

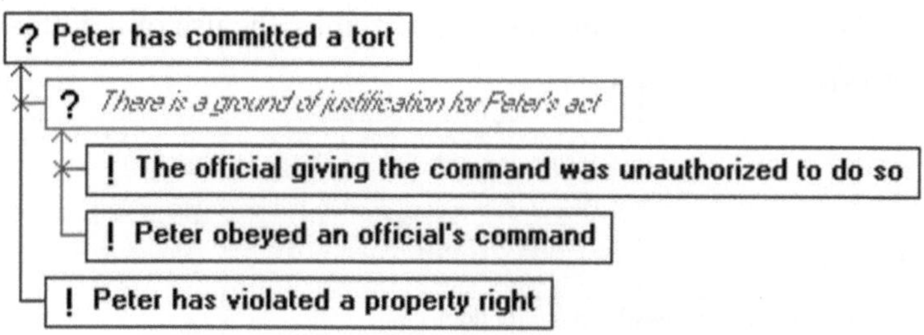

Figure 3.11: An exception that is not justified

If an exception is itself not justified, it has no undercutting effect. For instance, the argument in figure 3.11 is justifying.

Until now, the warrants of the steps and undercutters have been left implicit (cf., the discussion at the end of section 3.1.2). As long as the warrants of a dialectical argument are not at issue (but are instead implicitly assumed), they do not influence the justification status of the argument. If the warrants are at issue, they have effect on the justification status, as follows. If a step warrant statement is not justified, the conclusion of the step is not justified by the step's reason. Similarly, if an undercutter warrant is not justified, the corresponding undercutter has no effect (i.e., the undercutter's exception does not block the connection between reason and conclusion).

Figure 3.12: A step warrant that is not justified

For instance, in figure 3.12 an argument is shown that is not justifying because one of its steps is not warranted (in the sense that one of its step warrants is not justified). The argument is based on the opinion in the literature on Dutch tort law that bare violations of property rights are not torts by themselves (cf., e.g., Asser-Hartkamp 4-III 1998, Spier, Hartlief, Van Maanen and Vriesendorp 1997; see also Verheij, Hage and Van Maanen 1999). The fact that the step is unwarranted is visualized by the use of a dotted arrow.

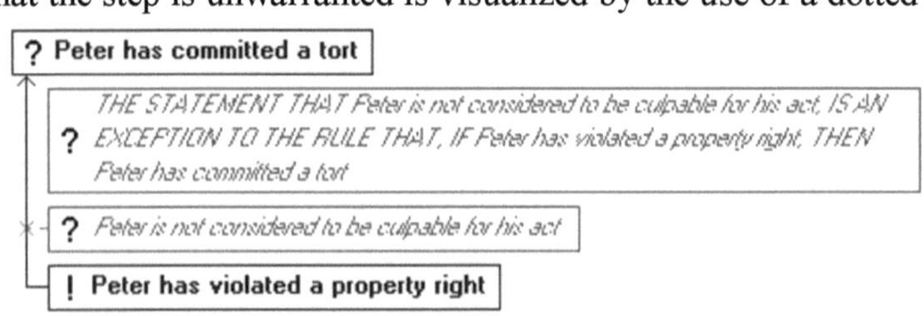

Figure 3.13: An undercutter warrant that is not justified

As said, an exception has no undercutting effect if the corresponding undercutter warrant is not justified. For instance, in the argument shown in figure 3.13, the statement that Peter is not held culpable for his act, occurs as an exception to the argument that Peter has committed a tort because of his violation of a property right. However, it has no effect since the corresponding undercutter warrant is an (unjustified) issue. In fact, justifying the undercutter warrant in this argument would be in conflict with actual Dutch tort law: the lack of culpability does not exclude that one has committed a tort, but can have an effect on the duty to repair the damages arising from the tort.

To summarize, whether a statement is justified, a reason is justifying, or an exception is undercutting, depends on the (recursive) structure of the argument in which it occurs (cf., section 3.1.2), and on the assumptions, as follows:

A statement is *justified* if
1. the statement is of the assumption type, or
2. the statement is of the issue type, and there is a reason justifying the statement.

Otherwise, the statement is not justified.

A reason *justifies* a conclusion if
a. the reason is justified, and
b. the corresponding step warrant statement is justified (or not made explicit), and
c. there is no exception undercutting the corresponding argument step.

Otherwise, the reason does not justify its conclusion.

An exception *undercuts* an argument step if
a. the exception is justified, and
b. the corresponding undercutter warrant statement is justified (or not made explicit).

Otherwise, the exception does not undercut an argument step.

This definition suffices for finite arguments (recall note 4).

3.2 THE GRIEVOUS BODILY HARM EXAMPLE

We now turn to the grievous bodily harm example (section 1.7), and will discuss its representation in ARGUMED 2.0. Figure 3.14 shows the same argumentative data as figure 2.2. The former is constructed in ARGUMED 2.0, the latter in ARGUE!.

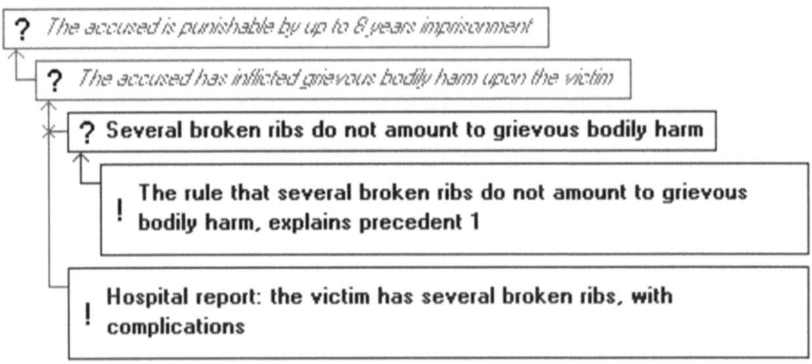

Figure 3.14: Adding an undercutting exception

In ARGUMED 2.0, it is possible to argue about the step warrant: why is the statement that the accused has inflicted grievous bodily harm upon the victim a reason for the conclusion that the accused is punishable by up to 8 years imprisonment? Figure 3.15 shows the argument why: in general, inflicting grievous bodily harm is punishable by up to 8 years imprisonment, and this is the case because of Article 302 Dutch criminal code.

The argumentation of the grievous bodily harm example cannot be continued in ARGUMED 2.0. For instance, in ARGUE! the statement that the accused has inflicted grievous bodily harm upon the victim could be attacked (on the basis of the accused's testimony; see figure 2.3). This has no counterpart in ARGUMED 2.0 since its argumentation theory only allows the attack of the connection between a reason and its conclusion. Another continuation of the argument that is not possible is the attack of the undercutter warrant: in the example, precedent 1 is not the most on point since it is a case of uncomplicated broken ribs while precedent 2 concerns broken ribs with complications.[6] As a result, it is possible to attack the defeating effect

---

[6] On-pointness is a notion that occurs in models of case-based reasoning in the law (see especially Ashley 1990). Roth (2003) provides a model of case-based reasoning in

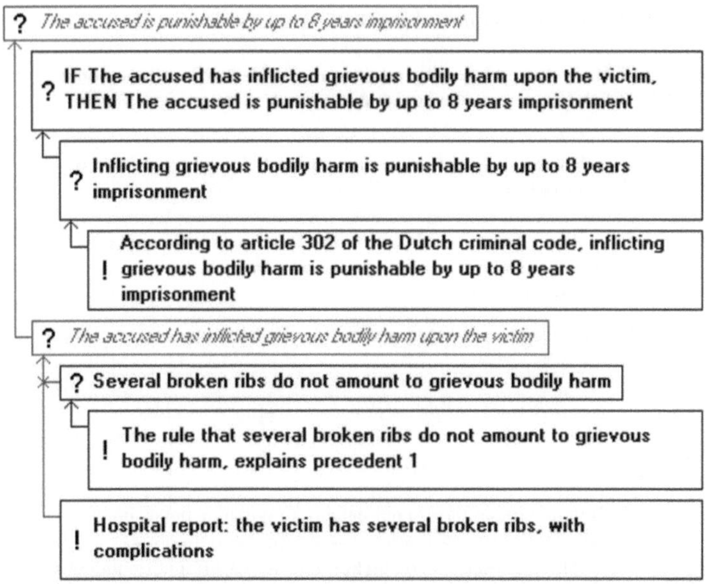

Figure 3.15: Justifying a step warrant

of the rule explaining precedent 1. In ARGUMED 2.0, the natural way would be an attack of the corresponding undercutter warrant. This is however impossible since ARGUMED 2.0's argumentation theory does not allow the attack of statements. In figure 3.16, the undercutter warrant ('THE STATEMENT THAT ...') is shown as an unsettled issue.

---

the law in which analogies between cases are established by comparing the dialectical structure of the arguments in cases. His dialectical arguments are inspired by the dialectical arguments of ArguMed.

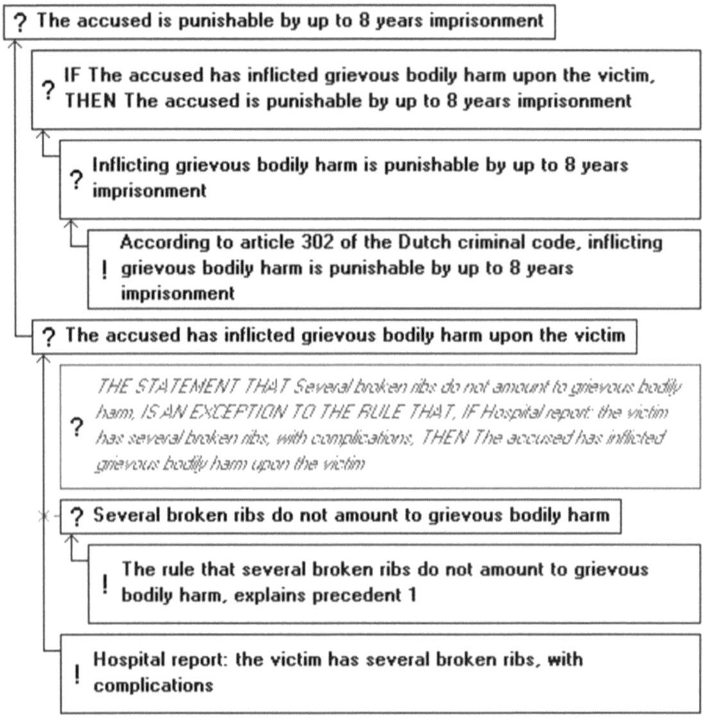

Figure 3.16: A non-justified undercutter warrant

3.3 PROGRAM DESIGN

3.3.1 Moves

There are three basic *argument moves*: making a statement, adding a reason and its conclusion, and providing an undercutting exception blocking the connection between a reason and its conclusion.

Each of the three 'Argue' buttons (see figure 3.17) gives access to one of the three argument *templates*, provided by the ARGUMED system, each corresponding to one of the argument moves of the system. To perform an argument move, the user fills in a form. The first template is the *statement template* (figure 3.18). It allows the input of a statement: the user can type a sentence and choose the statement's type. Statements can be of two types, viz., of the issue type and of the assumption type, cf., the distinction between issues and assumptions, as discussed in section 3.1.3. For new state-

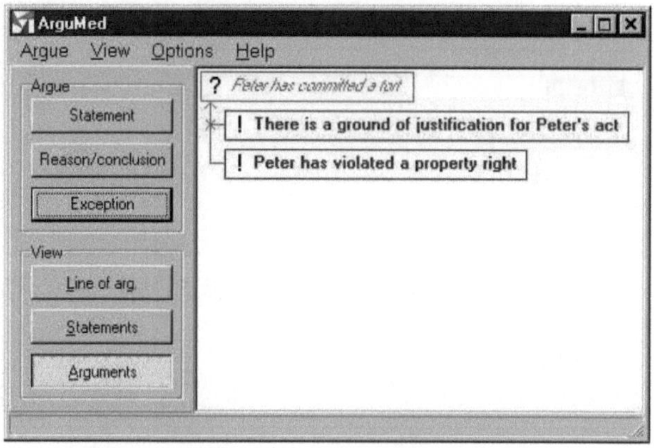

Figure 3.17: A sample screen

ments, the issue type is selected by default. The template can also be used to change the type of a statement added at a previous stage.

The second is the *reason/conclusion template*. It allows the input of a reason, and a conclusion supported by the reason. Both the reason and the conclusion can be new statements, or can be selected from statements added at a previous stage.

For a new conclusion, the issue type is selected by default; for a new reason, the assumption type. The intuition behind the latter default choice is that a reason is normally given as the immediate justification of a conclusion, and only a justified reason, such as a reason of the assumption type, can provide such support. If a reason is itself of the issue type, it can only indirectly justify its conclusion, viz., if the reason is supported by another (justified, non-blocked) reason.

By default, the step warrant corresponding to the reason/conclusion move is not made explicit. By selecting the appropriate box, the user can choose to add the step warrant as an issue or as an assumption.

The third is the *exception template*. It allows the input of an undercutting exception, and the reason and the conclusion, the connection of which is blocked by the exception. The user provides three statements, viz., the exception, the reason and the conclusion. Each of them can be new, or selected from the previously added statements.

For a new exception, the assumption type is selected by default. The intuition behind this choice is that an exception is normally meant as an

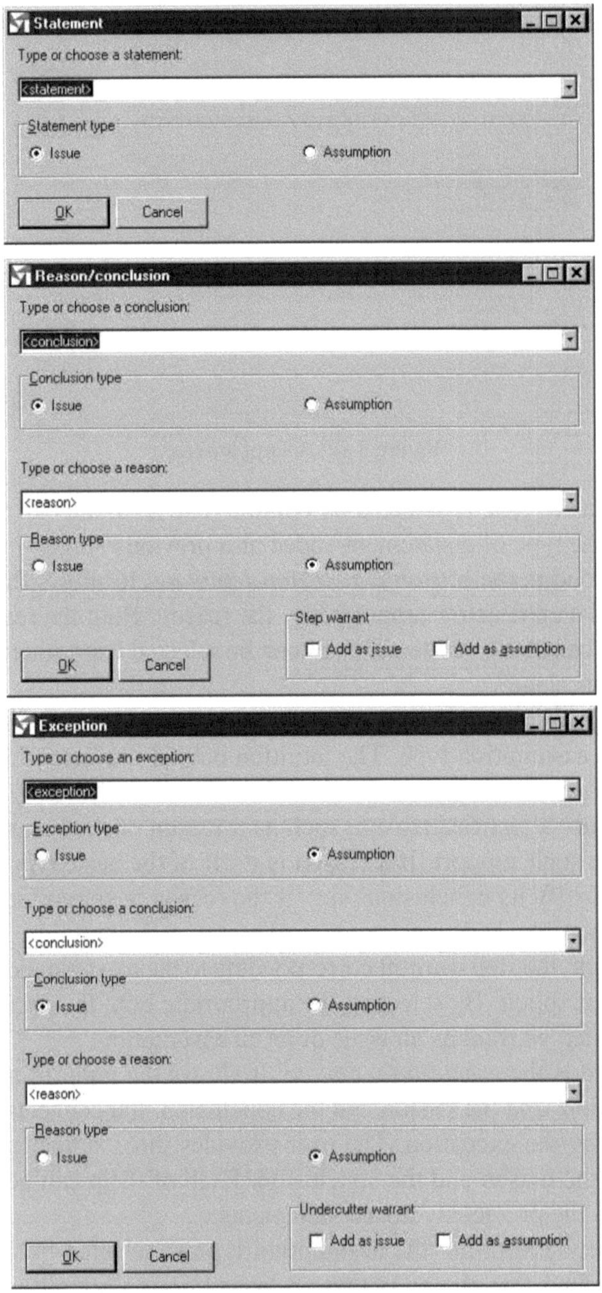

Figure 3.18: The three argument templates

immediate block of the connection between the reason and the conclusion, and only a justified exception is such a block. If the exception is of the issue type, it only blocks the connection between the reason and the conclusion if it is itself supported by a justified, non-blocked reason. For a new conclusion and reason, the default types are the same as in the reason/conclusion template.

By default, the undercutter warrant corresponding to the exception move is not made explicit. By selecting the appropriate box, the user can choose to add the undercutter warrant as an issue or as an assumption.

3.3.2 Views

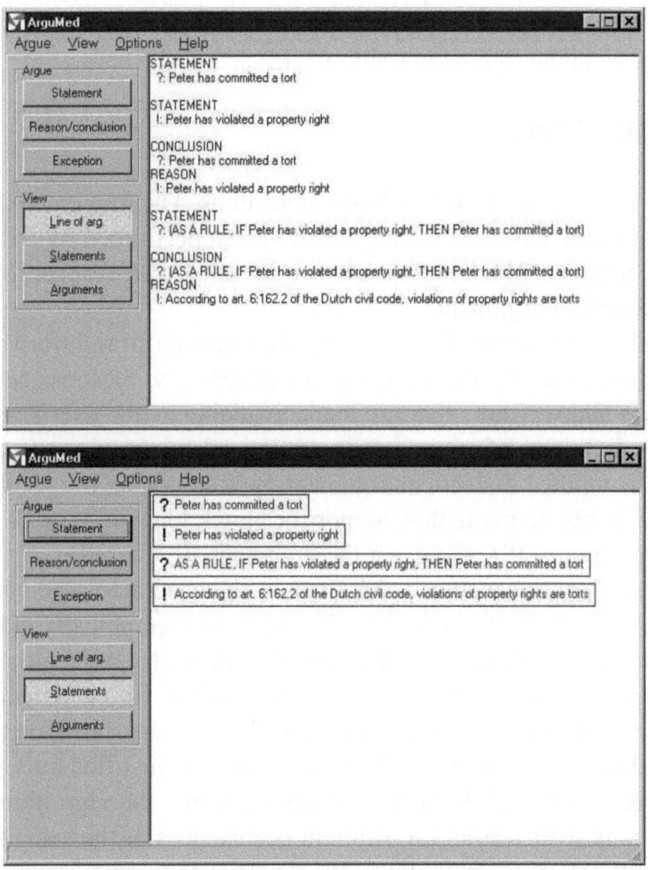

Figure 3.19: The 'line of argumentation' view and the 'statements' view

The ArguMed system has three *views*, providing information on the current argumentation session. Each view is accessible by one of the three 'View' buttons (see figure 3.17). In the 'line of argumentation' view, the argument moves are listed in the order in which they have been performed by the user (figure 3.19).

In the 'statements' view, all statements made by the user are presented. The type of the statements is visualized as follows: a question mark indicates a statement of the issue type, an exclamation mark a statement of the assumption type. Whether a statement is (currently) justified is shown by the use of coloured boxes and arrows, and different fonts (bold/italic).

In the 'arguments' view, the arguments that can be constructed on the basis of the current user input are shown. The arguments are shown as in the figures in section 3.1.3. Optionally, only the structure of the arguments is shown, as in the figures in section 3.1.2.

3.3.3 **Algorithms**

The ArguMed system has two basic algorithms. The first computes dialectical arguments, based on the argument moves performed by the user. The second computes which statements are justified with respect to the computed dialectical arguments.

The algorithm computing dialectical arguments straightforwardly constructs dialectical arguments using the statements, reasons, conclusions, exceptions and warrants that are made available by the user's moves. The recursive definition of arguments in section 3.1.2 is used.

Each computed dialectical argument makes maximum use of the available data; a restriction is that support or attack loops in (any branch of) a dialectical argument (as, e.g., in the argument '*P*. Therefore *Q*. Therefore *P*') are not further developed. As a result, the generated arguments are finite. In ArguMed 2.0, the break-off point is not graphically indicated (in contrast with ArguMed 3.0). The algorithm depends on the order in which the moves have been performed: e.g., the order in which statements have been adduced has effects on the order in which they are shown on the screen.

The algorithm computing which statements are justified follows the discussion in section 3.1.3. In case of attack loops, the algorithm does not provide consistent results for different occurrences of the same statement. An example is given in figure 3.20. (In ArguMed, one argument would appear below the other.) The statement 'a' undercuts 'd' as a reason for 'c', and 'c' undercuts 'b' as a reason for 'a'. The figure shows that loops are blocked off in the computation of dialectical arguments: for instance, in the argument on the left, the statement 'c' occurs twice, but only for one of them is the reason 'd' shown. The justification statuses are computed separately for the two dialectical arguments. For instance, in the argument on the left, 'a' is justified, but on the right it is not. Inside one dialectical argument, the statuses are computed per occurrence of a statement: when a statement occurs more than once its status depends on its position. For instance, the second occurrence of 'c' in the argument on the left (where it is an exception), is not justified since *at that position* it is an issue without a reason for it.

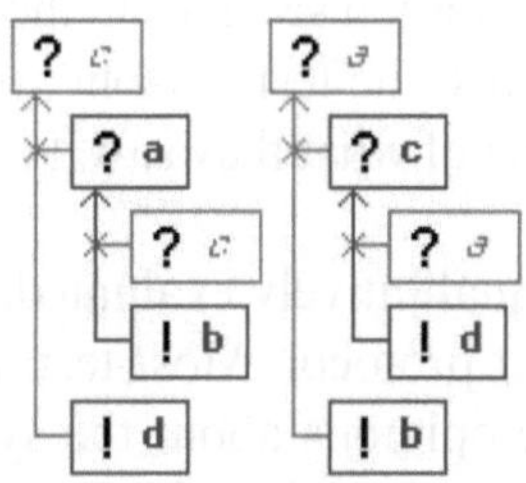

Figure 3.20: A loop of attacks in ARGUMED 2.0

The fact that in ARGUMED 2.0 the status of a statement is computed per occurrence of the statement is perhaps even more clear in the following example:

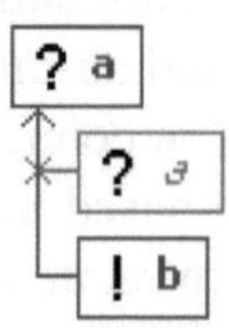

Figure 3.21: Self-attack in ARGUMED 2.0

From a logical point of view, it is unsatisfactory that different occurrences of the same statement can be evaluated differently. One of the purposes of the development of ARGUMED 3.0 was to build a system which does not have this drawback.

3.4 User Evaluation

ArguMed 2.0 was evaluated by a group of ten test persons. The group consisted of people from various backgrounds, mostly students and staff members of the Faculty of Law in Maastricht. They were asked to finish a test protocol containing several tasks to be performed within ArguMed 2.0. (The test protocol is available at <www.ai.rug.nl/~verheij/aaa/>. It is in Dutch however. Appendix A contains a translated excerpt.) The goal was to find out whether the system and its argumentation theory sufficiently spoke for themselves. For that purpose, the test protocol initially provided little information about the system's workings, but allowed the test persons to find out for themselves by showing unexplained examples and by asking them to try to reproduce argumentation samples in the system. Before explaining the argumentative structures, the test persons were asked to formulate hypotheses about the meaning of what they saw. (Cf., the excerpt of the protocol in Appendix A.)

The test results were qualitatively evaluated. Some test persons almost flawlessly finished the test protocol. Most test persons indicated that they had enjoyed the test. The opinions about the system were fairly positive. The opinions were more positive when the test protocol was finished more easily. The tests also showed a number of recurrent obstacles in the system and its argumentation theory. For instance, the dialectical arguments were understood fairly well, as long as there were no warrants involved. Not only was it difficult to reproduce warrants in the system, but also their intended role in argumentation was not entirely clear to all the test persons. The distinction between issues and assumptions turned out to be difficult for some test persons, especially in connection with the justification status of the statements. The template-based interface was not a complete success. For some, it was difficult to relate the slots of the templates to what was happening on the argument screen. Especially entering warrants was reported as being difficult. Several test persons expected that the argument screen would be mouse-sensitive, e.g., to repair small typing errors, but by trying they found out that it was not. A number of test persons reported the lack of a help function. The test persons also commented that it was not easy to repair typing errors or to delete a sentence.

In sum, the evaluation showed that a substantial part of ArguMed 2.0 and its argumentation theory required very little explanation and spoke for itself. However, this did not hold true for the distinction between issues and assumptions, the justification status of statements and the role of warrants. It can be expected that additional explanation and training will be helpful, especially since some test persons needed no further explanation at all. The evaluation also suggested that interaction with the argumentative data by template forms can be confusing.

Chapter 4
A Logical Extension: ArguMed 3.0 based on DefLog

Chapter 4
A Logical Extension: ArguMed 3.0 based on DefLog

ArguMed 3.0 is the successor of ArguMed 2.0. With respect to the program design, forms are no longer used for entering argumentative data. Instead, the screen has been made mouse-sensitive so that the user can interact directly with the argumentative data that is already shown. With respect to the argumentation theory, attack is no longer limited to undercutting exceptions, but it is possible to attack any statement. Moreover, the arrows used to represent support or attack are considered as conditional statements, which allows a natural treatment of warrants and undercutters. The argumentation theory corresponds to DefLog, a logical theory of prima facie justified assumptions.

4.1 Argumentation Theory

The argumentation theory of ArguMed 3.0 is an extension and streamlining of that of ArguMed 2.0. Whereas in ArguMed 2.0 the focus was on undercutters, i.e., attacking the connection between a reason and its conclusion, ArguMed 3.0 allows an attack on all statements.

4.1.1 The structure of dialectical arguments

In ArguMed 3.0, dialectical arguments consist of statements that can have two types of connection between them: a statement can *support* another, or a statement can *attack* another. The former is indicated by a pointed arrow between statements, the latter by an arrow ending in a cross. Here is an example:

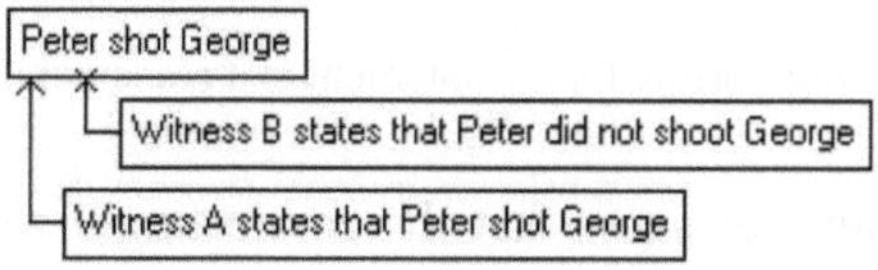

Figure 4.1: Support and attack

The dialectical argument consists of three elementary statements, viz., that Peter shot George, that witness A states that Peter shot George, and that witness B states that Peter did not shoot George. As indicated, the second is a reason supporting that Peter shot George, the third a reason attacking that Peter shot George.

The expressiveness of dialectical arguments is significantly enhanced by considering the connecting arrows (of both the supporting and the attacking type) as a kind of statement, that can as such be supported and attacked. The arrow of a supporting or attacking argument step is here called the conditional underlying the step.

For instance, one could ask why A's testimony supports that Peter shot George. In the following, the statement that witness testimonies are often truthful is adduced as a reason:

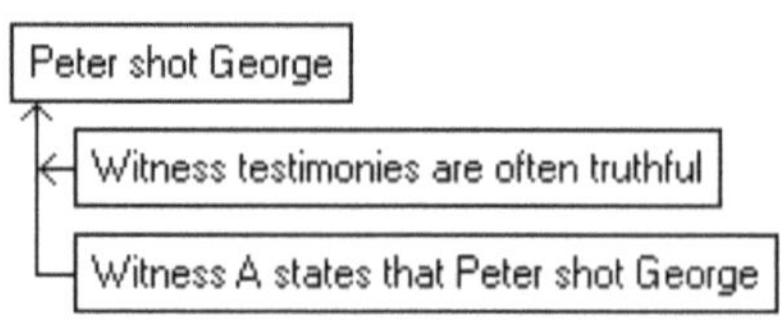

Figure 4.2: Supporting that a statement is a reason for another

The statement that witness testimonies are often truthful serves as reason why it follows from A's testimony that Peter shot George. The same statement can back the attacking argument step of B's testimony attacking that Peter shot George.

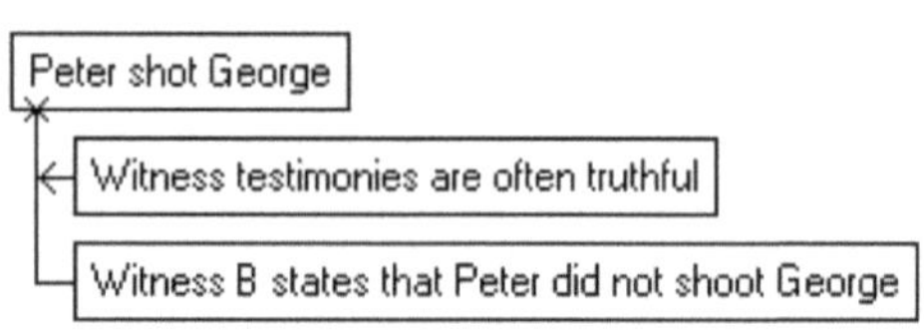

Figure 4.3: Supporting that a statement is a reason against another

The following examples show that the connecting arrows can also be attacked:

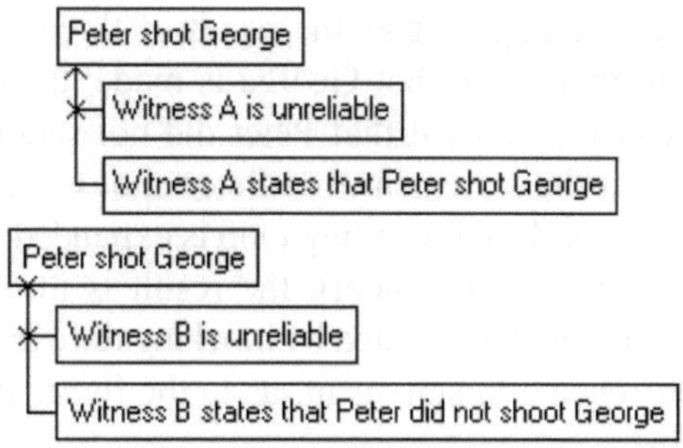

Figure 4.4: Attacking that a statement is a reason

Here the unreliability of witnesses A and B, respectively, are adduced as reasons against the consequential effect of their testimonies.

In general, dialectical arguments are finite structures that result from a finite number of applications of three kinds of construction types:

1. Making a statement
2. Supporting a previously made statement by a reason for it
3. Attacking a previously made statement by a reason against it

It should be borne in mind that types two and three consist of making two statements: one an ordinary elementary statement, viz., the reason for or against a statement, the other the special statement that the reason and the supported or attacked statement are connected, as expressed by the conditional underlying the supporting or attacking argument step.

Though dialectical arguments are here considered as the result of a finite construction, their corresponding tree structure can be virtually infinite. An example is given in the following picture:

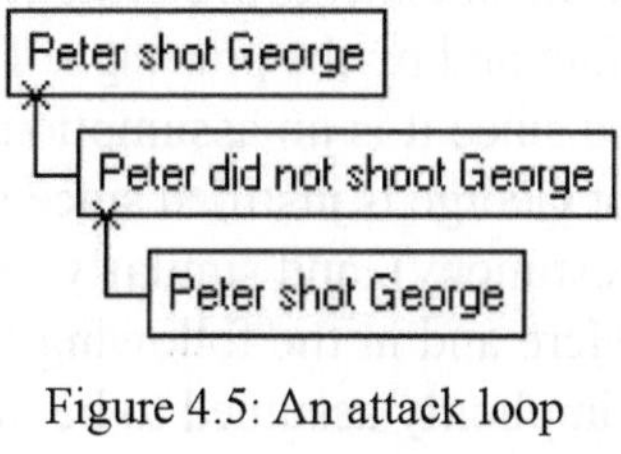

Figure 4.5: An attack loop

The dots indicate where the argument could be further extended.

The argument can be thought of as the result of three construction steps. First, the statement that Peter shot George is made, then that statement is attacked by the reason against it that Peter did not shoot George, and, finally, it is stated that the statement that Peter shot George is in its turn a reason against its attack. If the resulting loop is expanded as a tree (growing downward from the initial statement), the result is infinite. The relevant information can be finitely represented by blocking the expansion of a branch after the first recurrence of a statement, as in the figure (which was generated by the system).

4.1.2 Evaluating dialectical arguments

Dialectical arguments can be evaluated with respect to a set of prima facie justified assumptions. An example of an evaluated dialectical argument is the following:

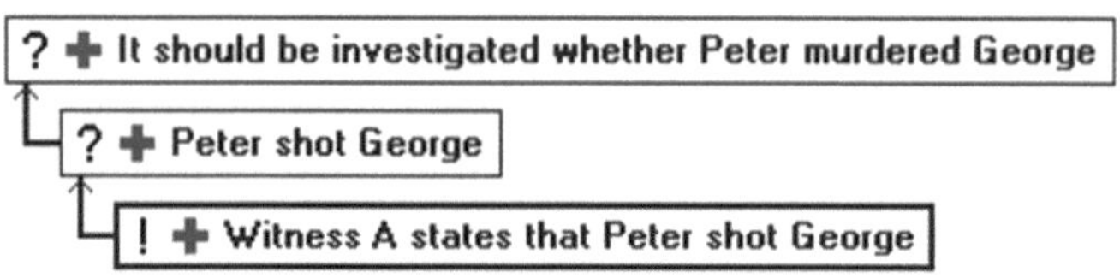

Figure 4.6: An evaluated argument

Like in ArguMed 2.0, assumptions are preceded by an exclamation mark, all others – called issues – by a question mark. Another way to distinguish assumptions from issues is that assumptions are represented using thicker lines. For instance, in figure 4.6, the statement that witness A states that Peter shot George is an assumption, while the other two statements shown are issues. The three shown statements are evaluated as justified, as is indicated by the dark bold font and by the plus sign. The statement concerning A's testimony is justified since it is an assumption that is not attacked; the statement that Peter shot George is justified since it is supported by a justifying reason (viz., A's testimony), and similarly for the statement concerning the investigation. (Here and in the following the conditionals underlying argument steps are implicitly assumed to be prima facie justified.)

The following example involves an attack against the support relation between two statements:

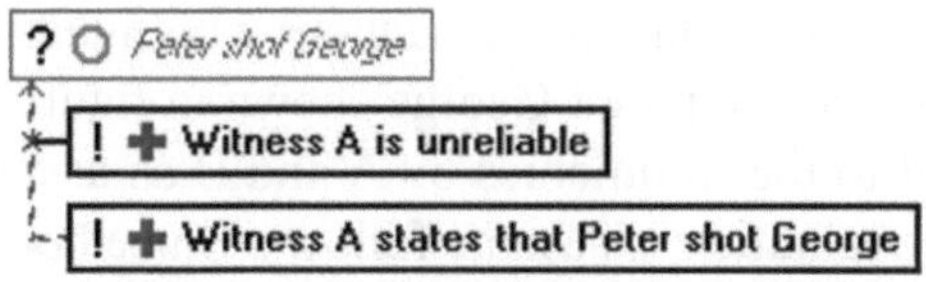

Figure 4.7: An evaluated dialectical argument

The statements concerning A's testimony and unreliability are assumptions, while the statement that Peter shot George is an issue. The two assumptions are justified since they are not attacked. The statement that Peter shot George is unevaluated (as is indicated by the light italic font and the zero sign): it is not justified or defeated since it is an issue without a justifying or defeating reason.

An example of a dialectical argument in which a statement is defeated is the following:

Figure 4.8: A defeated assumption

The assumption that Peter shot George is defeated (as is indicated by the bold font and the cross sign) since it is attacked by the reason against it that witness B states that Peter did not shoot George.

The evaluation of dialectical arguments with respect to a set of prima facie justified assumptions is naturally constrained as follows:

1. A statement is *justified* if, and only if,
   a. it is an assumption, against which there is no defeating reason, or
   b. it is an issue, for which there is a justifying reason.

   A statement is *defeated* if, and only if, there is a defeating reason against it.
2. A reason is *justifying* if, and only if, the reason and the conditional underlying the corresponding supporting argument step are justified.
3. A reason is *defeating* if, and only if, the reason and the conditional underlying the corresponding attacking argument step are justified.

It is a fundamental complication of dialectical argumentation that a dialectical argument can have any number of evaluations with respect to a set of prima facie justified assumptions: there can be no evaluation, or one, or several.

Assuming, as we do, that statements cannot be both justified and defeated, the argument whether Peter shot George shown in figure 4.1 has no evaluation with respect to the testimonies by A and B as assumptions. That the argument has no evaluation is seen as follows. Since both assumptions are not attacked they must be justified in every evaluation. But then A's testimony would require that it is justified that Peter shot George, while at the same time B's testimony would require that it is defeated that Peter shot George. This is impossible.

An example of a dialectical argument with two evaluations is the looping argument discussed above:

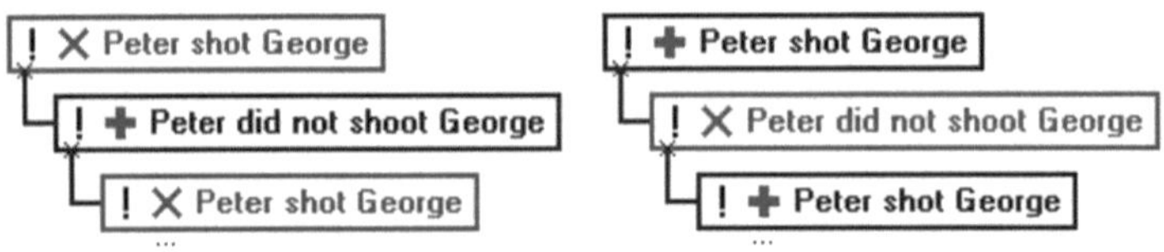

Figure 4.9: An example with two evaluations

The argument has two prima facie justified assumptions, viz., that Peter shot George and that Peter did not shoot George. The assumptions attack each other. In one evaluation, it is justified that Peter shot George, thus defeating that Peter did not shoot George, while in the other evaluation it is the other way around.

Note that the existence of the two evaluations is possible because the loop of attacks consists of an even number of statements. An odd length loop of attacks can result in the nonexistence of an evaluation. Two examples – inspired by the liar's paradox (cf., for instance Gamut 1991, p. 10) – are shown in figure 4.10:

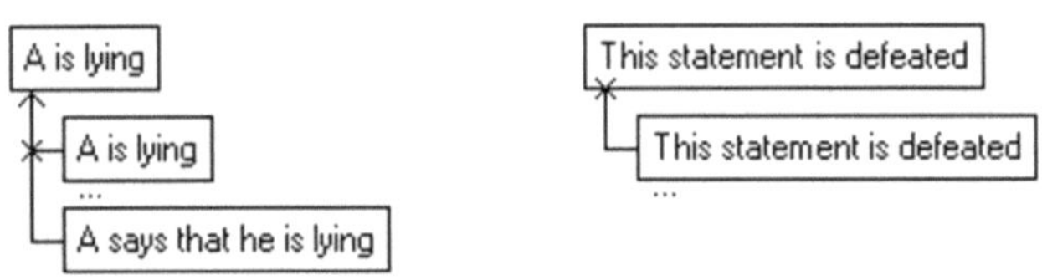

Figure 4.10: Two examples in which there is no evaluation

In the example on the left, there are three assumptions. The first is that A says that he is lying. The second (represented by the supporting arrow) is that A's saying that he is lying supports that he is lying. The third (represented by the attacking arrow) is that when A is lying. A's saying that he is lying provides no support for A's lying. By reasoning that is well-known from all variants of the liar's paradox it follows that there is no evaluation.[1] The example on the right with a self-attacking assumption is similar.[2]

4.1.3 When can argumentation end?

The theory of dialectical argumentation sketched above can be used to formulate heuristics for legal decision making. Such heuristics should prescribe when (for instance) a judge can stop his line of argumentation and when he needs to continue it in order to reach a better decision.

When can a line of argumentation stop? Four questions need to be answered in the affirmative:[3]

1. *Is any (justified) assumption sufficiently obvious?*
   If not, the assumption should be turned into an issue, and requires support of its own. In the situation of a criminal court, statements taken literally from a testimony or from a police report, can often serve as sufficiently obvious assumptions. Notice that their obviousness does not imply that they are justified: since assumptions are defeasible, they are not immune to counterarguments. Other examples of sufficiently obvious assumptions include generally agreed upon facts and rules. In the final dialectical argument above, the statement that witnesses A and B are unreliable is an example of a statement that is not sufficiently obvious and requires further support. It should therefore be turned into an issue.

---

[1] Assume that there is an evaluation. If the statement that A is lying were justified in the evaluation, it would have to be justified by A's saying that he is lying. However, that is impossible since the statement that A is lying then attacks the supporting connection. The statement that A is lying cannot be defeated either since it is not attacked. But when the statement that A is lying is neither justified nor defeated in the evaluation, A's saying that he is lying justifies that A is lying, contradicting the statement that it is not justified that A is lying. By reductio ad absurdum it follows that there is no evaluation.

[2] Note that for DEFLOG the statement 'This statement is defeated' is taken as an elementary statement, just like 'John is a thief' or 'p'. DEFLOG's language does not include a demonstrative 'this' nor does it contain a predicate 'is defeated'. Cf., section 4.1.4.

[3] A precondition for stopping a line of argumentation is here that the dialectical argument or arguments can be uniquely evaluated with respect to the assumptions. For present purposes, this precondition is not further discussed.

2. *For any justifying or defeating statement, is it clear why it is at all supporting or attacking?*
   If not, backing the argument step is required. A reference to a general rule phrased in a legal code or precedent can serve well as the backing of an argument step. An example of an argument step that needs further backing can be found in the final dialectical argument above: it is worthwhile making explicit that policemen's testimonies are often truthful.
3. *For any statement that is not justified, have all statements that can support it been adduced as reasons?*
   If not, the additional reasons should be adduced. Even prima facie reasons that are considered to be not justifying, should be adduced, since it is informative to make explicit why it is non-justifying. It can turn out, for instance, that there is no backing or that there is an undercutting exception.
4. *For any statement that is not defeated, have all statements that can attack it been adduced as counterarguments?*
   If not, the additional counterarguments should be adduced. Also non-defeating counterarguments should be adduced in order to make explicit why it is not defeating. For instance, there could be a counter-counterargument or no backing.

Each of the actions prescribed when a question is answered negatively, can lead to changes in the evaluation. For instance, if an assumption is turned into an issue, and there is no justifying reason for it, it will no longer be justified. If a statement is not defeated, while a new counterargument is adduced, the statement can become defeated.

Essentially, the heuristics have the effect that argumentation can stop when a single argumentative move does not lead to a better theory concerning the case (i.e., the set of prima facie assumptions).[4]

The main sources of information that can or even should be used in answering the four questions, are the law (as, e.g., laid down in legal codes, treaties, and precedents), the case materials (e.g., testimonies by witnesses and experts, police reports and court pleadings) and the decision maker's own knowledge and experience.

---

[4] This shows a connection with the comparison of theories in coherentist views of justification. Cf., (in the field of AI & law) Bench-Capon and Sartor (2001) and Hage (2001a).

If all four questions are answered in the affirmative, the line of argumentation can stop, and the statements justified therein can be regarded as a good decision from the point of view of the theory of dialectical argumentation. It should be noted that the resulting evaluation of the decision is not an absolute notion. Additional or deviating insights or information can change the answers to the four questions, and can require a continuation of the line of argumentation. For instance, new information can show that there is an unthought of reason or exception.

As a result, the 'dialectical structure' of a legal decision is not only a tool for the legal decision maker, but also for his challengers, i.e., the prosecution, the defence, and a court of appeal. All can answer the questions for themselves, and thus find clues for undermining or strengthening the argumentation.

4.1.4 DEFLOG: a theory of prima facie justified assumptions

The ideas on dialectical argumentation discussed above can be made formally precise in terms of the logical system DEFLOG (Verheij 2000a, 2003a). See also Appendix B.

The dialectical interpretation of theories

DEFLOG's starting point is a simple logical language with two connectives $\times$ and $\leadsto$. The first is a unary connective that is used to express the defeat of a statement, the latter is a binary connective that is used to express that one statement supports another. When φ and ψ are sentences, then $\times\varphi$ (φ's so-called *dialectical negation*) expresses that the statement φ is defeated, and $(\varphi \leadsto \psi)$ that the statement φ supports the statement ψ. Attack, denoted as $\rtimes$, is defined in terms of these two connectives: $\varphi \rtimes \psi$ is defined as $\varphi \leadsto \times\psi$, and expresses that the statement φ attacks the statement ψ, or equivalently that φ supports the defeat of ψ. When p, q, r and s are elementary sentences, then $p \leadsto (q \leadsto r)$, $p \leadsto \times(q \leadsto \times r)$ and $(p \leadsto q) \leadsto (p \leadsto \times(r \leadsto s))$ are some examples of sentences. For the sake of convenience, outer brackets will be omitted.

The central definition of DEFLOG is its notion of the *dialectical interpretation* of a theory. Formally, DEFLOG's dialectical interpretations of theories are a variant of Reiter's (1980) extensions of default theories, Gelfond and Lifschitz's (1988) stable models of logic programming, Dung's (1995) stable extensions of argumentation frameworks, and Bondarenko et al.'s (1997) stable extensions of assumption-based frameworks.[5]

A theory is any set of sentences, and when it is dialectically interpreted, all sentences in the theory are evaluated, either as justified or as defeated. (This is in contrast to the interpretation of theories in standard logic, where all sentences in an interpreted theory are assigned the same positive value, namely true, e.g., by providing a model of the theory.)

An assignment of the values justified or defeated to the sentences in a theory gives rise to a dialectical interpretation of the theory, when two conditions are fulfilled. First, the justified part of the theory must be conflict-free. Second, the justified part of the theory must attack all sentences in the defeated part. Formally the definitions are as follows.

(i) Let T be a set of sentences and φ a sentence. Then T *supports* φ when φ is in T or follows from T by the repeated application of $\rightsquigarrow$-Modus ponens (i.e., from $\varphi \rightsquigarrow \psi$ and φ, conclude ψ). T *attacks* φ when T supports $\times\varphi$.

(ii) Let T be a set of sentences. Then T is *conflict-free* when there is no sentence φ that is both supported and attacked by T.

(iii) Let Δ be a set of sentences, and let J and D be subsets of Δ that have no elements in common and that have Δ as their union. Then (J, D) *dialectically interprets* the theory Δ when J is conflict-free and attacks all sentences in D. The sentences in J are the *justified statements* of the theory Δ, the sentences in D the *defeated statements*.

(iv) Let Δ be a set of sentences and let (J, D) dialectically interpret the theory Δ. Then (Supp(J), Att(J)) is a *dialectical interpretation* or *ex-*

---

[5] In appendix B, a formal connection with Dung's (1995) work is established. More relations between the formalisms mentioned are for instance discussed by Dung (1995) and in the extended manuscript on DefLog (Verheij 2000a). To guide intuition, the following may be useful. A default p : q / r (as in Reiter's 1980) would in DefLog be translated as two conditionals, viz., $p \rightsquigarrow r$ and $\neg q \rightsquigarrow \times(p \rightsquigarrow r)$. The second says that the former is defeated in case of $\neg q$. This corresponds to the intuition underlying the default that r follows from p as long as q can consistently be assumed. (Note, however, that the properties of ordinary negation $\neg$ are not part of DefLog.) A rule in logic programming $p \leftarrow q, \sim r$ (where $\sim$ is negation as failure) corresponds in DefLog to two conditionals, viz., $q \rightsquigarrow p$ and $r \rightsquigarrow \times(q \rightsquigarrow p)$. The second says that $q \rightsquigarrow p$ is defeated in case of r. This corresponds to the intuition underlying the program rule that p follows when q is proven, while r is not. For the technical details, the reader is referred to Verheij (2000a).

tension of the theory Δ. Here Supp(J) denotes the set of sentences supported by J, and Att(J) the set of sentences attacked by J. The sentences in Supp(J) are the *justified statements* of the dialectical interpretation, the sentences in Att(J) the *defeated statements*.

Note that when (J, D) dialectically interprets Δ and (Supp(J), Att(J)) is the corresponding dialectical interpretation, J is equal to Supp(J) ∩ Δ, and D to Att(J) ∩ Δ. It is convenient to say that a dialectical interpretation (Supp(J), Att(J)) of a theory Δ *is specified by* J.

The examples discussed in sections 4.1.1 and 4.1.2 can be used to illustrate these definitions. Let the sentence s express Peter's shooting of George, a A's testimony, b B's testimony, t the truthfulness of testimonies, u A's unreliability, and i the obligation to investigate. Then the example shown in figure 4.6 corresponds to the three-sentence theory {a, a ⇝ s, s ⇝ i}. The arrows in the figure correspond to the two conditional sentences. The theory has a unique extension in which all statements of the theory are justified. In the extension, two other statements are justified, viz., s and i. The example in figure 4.8 corresponds to the theory {b, b ⇝ ×s, s}. The arrow ending in a cross in the figure corresponds to the sentence b ⇝ ×s. The theory is not conflict-free, but has a unique extension in which b and b ⇝ ×s are justified, while s is defeated. In the extension, there is one other interpreted statement, viz. ×s, which is justified. The example of figure 4.2 corresponds to the theory {a, t, t ⇝ (a ⇝ s)}. In its unique extension, all statements of the theory are justified, and in addition a ⇝ s and s. The example of figure 4.7 corresponds to the theory {a, u, u ⇝ ×(a ⇝ s)}. In its unique extension, a ⇝ s is defeated and s is not interpreted (i.e., neither justified nor defeated). Note that the theory {a, u, u ⇝ ×(a ⇝ s), a ⇝ s} has the same unique extension, but is not conflict-free.

DEFLOG's logical language only uses two connectives, viz., ⇝ and ×. Notwithstanding its simple structure, many central notions of dialectical argumentation can be analyzed in terms thereof. For instance, it is possible to define an inconclusive conditional (i.e., a conditional for which the consequent does not always follow when its antecedent holds true) in terms of DEFLOG's defeasible conditional (that is defeasible in the same way as any other statement). Other examples of DEFLOG's expressiveness are Toulmin's (1958) warrants and backings and Pollock's (1987) undercutting and rebutting defeaters. Verheij (2000a) discusses how to express these notions.

Theories without and with several extensions

The examples of theories discussed above all had a unique extension. Several were examples of the following general property: a conflict-free theory always has a unique extension, namely the extension specified by the theory itself. The simplest example of a theory that is not conflict-free with a unique extension is {p, ×p}. In the theory's extension, p is defeated and ×p justified. Other important examples of theories that are not conflict-free, but do have a unique extension are {p, q, q ⇝ ×p} and {p, q, r, q ⇝ ×p, r ⇝ ×q}. In the former theory, the statement that p is attacked by the statement that q. In its unique extension, q and ×p are justified and p is defeated. The latter theory is a superset of the former: in addition to q's attack of p, r attacks q. In its unique extension, p, ×q and r are justified, and q is defeated. The theories together provide an example of *reinstatement*: a statement is first defeated, since it is attacked by a counterargument, but becomes justified by the addition of a counterattack, i.e., an attack against the counterargument. Here p is reinstated: it is first successfully attacked by q, but the attack is then countered by r attacking q.

There are, however, also theories with no or with several extensions:

(i) The three theories {p, p ⇝ ×p}, {p, p ⇝ q, ×q} and {p_i | i is a natural number} ∪ {p_j ⇝ ×p_i | i and j are natural numbers, such that $i < j$} lack extensions. For the latter theory, this can be seen as follows. Assume that there is an extension E in which p_n is justified for some natural number n. Then all p_m with $m > n$ must be defeated in E, for if such a p_m were justified, p_n could not be justified. But that is impossible, for the defeat of a p_m with $m > n$ can only be the result of an attack by a justified $p_{m'}$ with $m' > m$. As a result, no p_i can be justified in E. But then all p_i must be defeated in E, which is impossible since the defeat of a p_i can only be the result of an attack by a justified p_j with $j > i$. (Note that any *finite* subset of the latter theory has an extension, while the whole theory does not. This shows a 'non-compactness' property[6] of extensions.)

---

[6] A property P of sets is called compact if a set S has property P whenever all its finite subsets have this property P. Cf., the compactness of satisfiability in first-order predicate logic.

(ii) The three theories $\{p, q, p \rightsquigarrow \times q, q \rightsquigarrow \times p\}$, $\{p_i, p_{i+1} \rightsquigarrow \times p_i \mid i \text{ is a natural number}\}$ and $\{\times^i p \mid i \text{ is a natural number}\}$ have two extensions. Here $\times^i p$ denotes, for any natural number i, the sentence composed of a length i sequence of the connective $\times$, followed by the constant p. (Note that each finite subset of the latter theory has a unique extension, showing another non-compactness property.)

4.2 THE GRIEVOUS BODILY HARM EXAMPLE

ARGUE! and ARGUMED 2.0 could not represent the same argumentation concerning the grievous bodily harm example of section 1.7. Whereas ARGUE! allowed the attack of statements, which ARGUMED 2.0 did not, ARGUE! could not deal with the warrants underlying argument steps. ARGUMED 3.0 combines the strong points of both.

Figure 4.11 integrates the argumentative data represented in figure 2.3 (made with ARGUE!) and in figure 3.15 (taken from ARGUMED 2.0).

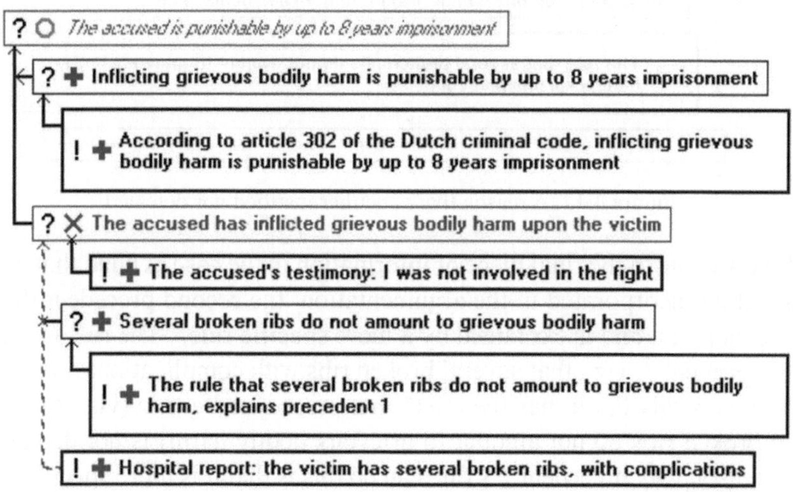

Figure 4.11: A defeated reason

In figure 4.11, the conclusion that the accused is punishable is not justified since the only reason for this (the inflicting of grievous bodily harm) is not justified, and is even defeated, namely by the accused's testimony.

In the case at hand, there is further information that makes the accused's testimony non-defeating: the testimonies of 10 pub customers that the accused was indeed involved in the fight. Figure 4.12 shows how the argument is extended to incorporate this information. Still, there is no reason justifying the punishability of the accused, but the prima facie reason that the accused has inflicted grievous bodily harm has become unevaluated instead of defeated.

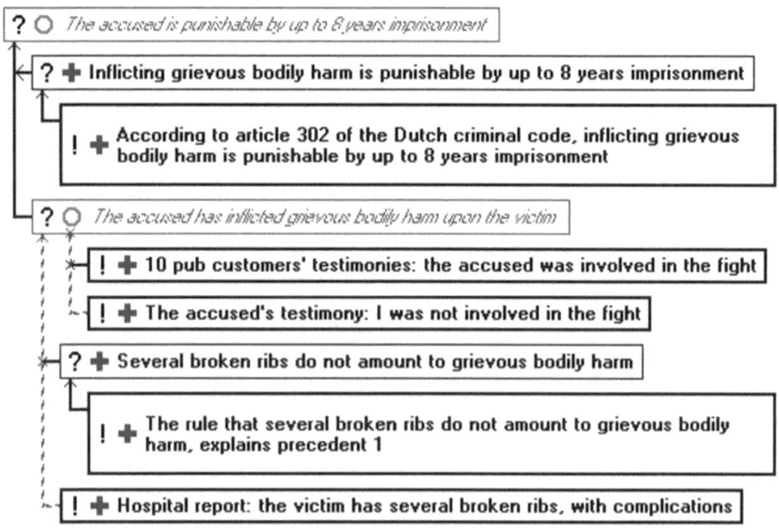

Figure 4.12: A reason that is neither justified nor defeated

We now come to the final piece of information in the case at hand that could not yet be incorporated in the argumentation: the second precedent that is more on point, and is explained by a more specific rule.[7] The rule explaining precedent 2, viz., that several broken ribs with complications amount to grievous bodily harm, has the effect that precedent 1's rule (viz., that several broken ribs do not amount to grievous bodily harm) is not defeating. The reason why precedent 2's rule can do this is that it is more specific. The result is shown in figure 4.13. In the end, the conclusion that the accused is

[7] For details about the formal modelling of case-based reasoning in the law, the reader can for instance consult the work of Ashley (1990) and Roth (2003). See also note 6 of chapter 3.

punishable by up to 8 years imprisonment is justified by the reason that he has inflicted grievous bodily harm upon the victim.

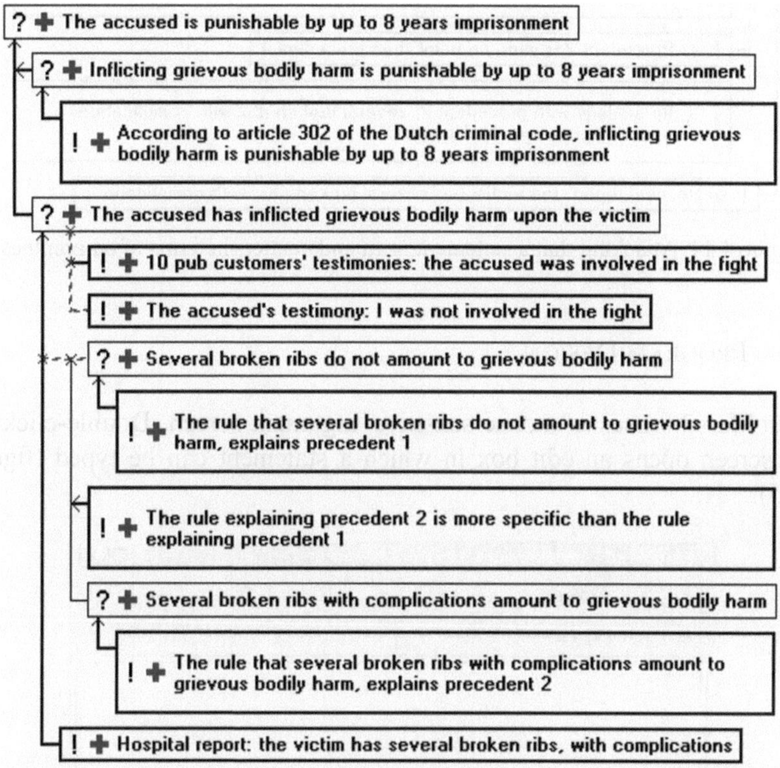

Figure 4.13: Attacking that a statement is an undercutter

A variant of the precedent-based reasoning is shown in figure 4.14. It makes explicit that precedent 2 is more on point than precedent 1. The argumentation could continue by justifying why this is the case: the reason would be that precedent 2 shares more factors with the current case than precedent 1 since precedent 2 concerns a case of broken ribs with complications, and complications are a relevant factor.

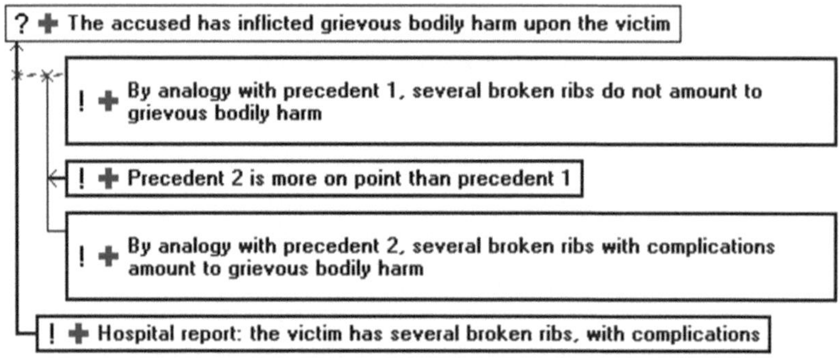

Figure 4.14: Attacking that a statement is an undercutter (in terms of on-pointness)

4.3 Program Design

ArguMed 3.0 uses a 'mouse-sensitive' argument screen. Double-clicking the screen opens an edit box in which a statement can be typed (figure 4.15).

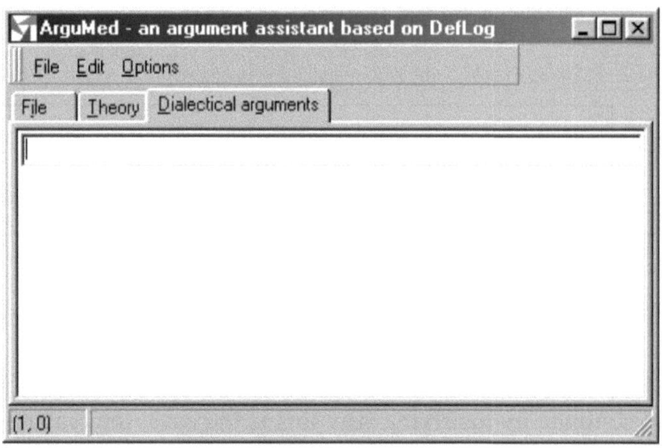

Figure 4.15: Adding a statement

Further argumentative data can be added using the context menu that appears after right-clicking the mouse on a statement or an arrow (figure 4.16).

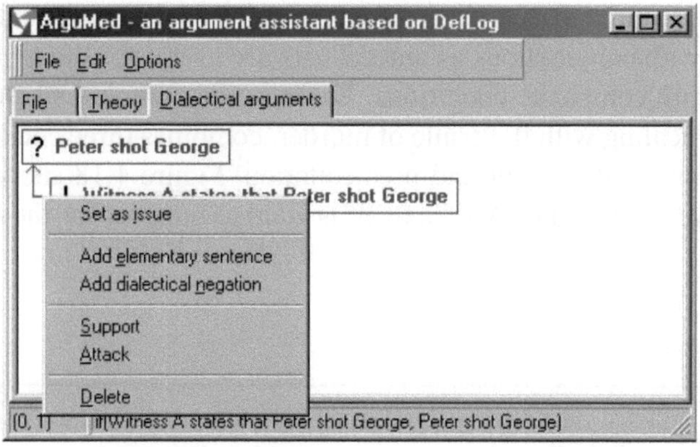

Figure 4.16: Editing the argumentative data

Recently, a toolbar has been added (Figure 4.17). Argument moves can be made by clicking one of the buttons. The toolbar is context-sensitive: only those buttons that allow moves pertaining to the active statement can be clicked. For instance, when the active statement is an issue, the 'Set as issue' button cannot be clicked, while the 'Set as assumption' button is available. There are buttons for adding an elementary statement, for setting a statement as an assumption or as an issue, to support or attack a statement, and to add a conjunct. Note that the use of buttons in ARGUMED and in ARGUE! is different: the latter change the graphical mode (such as the mode of drawing an arrow), while the former correspond to argument moves (such as supporting a statement).

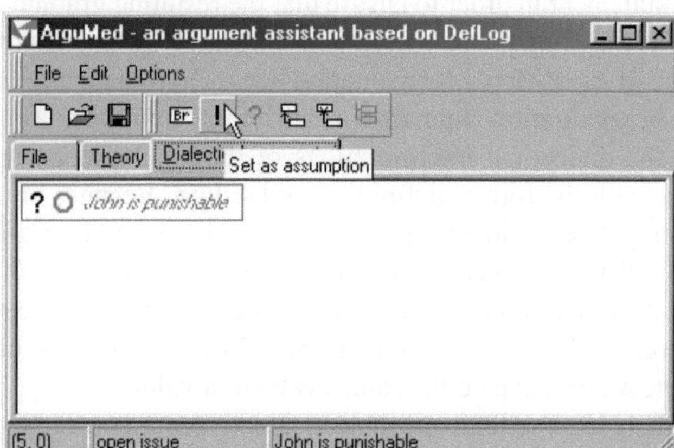

Figure 4.17: Using the toolbar

Adding a conjunct to a conditional statement was not yet encountered. Conditionals with conjunctions as antecedents are useful for the representation of rules with composite conditions. For instance, Article 289 Dutch criminal code, dealing with the crime of murder, combines three conditions: taking someone's life, intent and premeditation. Figure 4.18 shows how this can be represented. The Article itself is cited as support for the conditional statement.

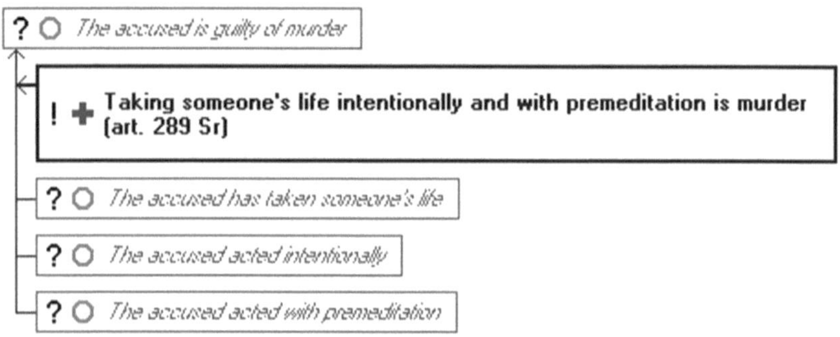

Figure 4.18: A conditional statement with a conjunction as antecedent

In ArguMed 3.0, dialectical arguments are computed starting from the conclusion, by recursively adding the reasons for and against the statements in the argument (including the connecting conditionals). When a branch of the argument contains a loop, the recursion stops after the first repeated occurrence of a statement in order to ensure that the resulting graphical structure is finite. The blocking of the recursion is indicated by a series of dots (...).

Just like in ArguMed 2.0, evaluation occurs automatically in the background. The evaluation algorithm is different, however: ArguMed 3.0 computes the dialectical interpretations of the available assumptions, in accordance with the formal definitions of DefLog. Because of this logical underpinning, from a logical point of view, the evaluation algorithm of ArguMed 3.0 is more satisfactory than that of ArguMed 2.0. One may recall that the latter could evaluate different occurrences of the same statement differently. This is not the case in ArguMed 3.0: different occurrences of a statement are assigned the same evaluation value.

When there is more than one dialectical interpretation, each of them can be viewed. Figure 4.19 shows two evaluated dialectical arguments corresponding to the two different dialectical interpretations of the same set of assumptions. When there is no dialectical interpretation, all statements are shown as being unevaluated (figure 4.20).

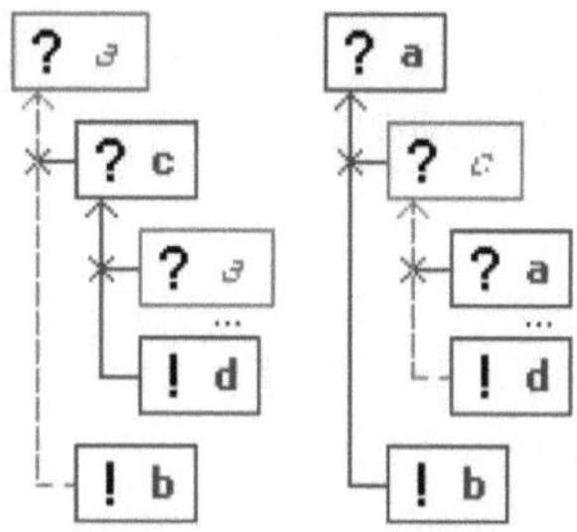

Figure 4.19: Two dialectical interpretations

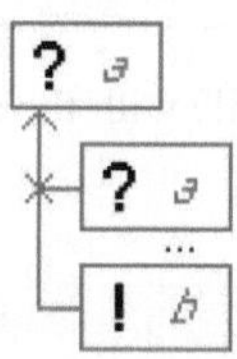

Figure 4.20: No dialectical interpretation

ARGUMED 3.0 has three viewing screens. The first shows the file that contains the argumentative data (figure 4.21). It is formatted in an XML-styled format. The second lists the prima facie justified assumptions (figure 4.22). The third shows the dialectical arguments as evaluated in accordance with the assumptions' dialectical interpretations (figure 4.23). If applicable, the different dialectical interpretations can be viewed by clicking a corresponding dynamically-generated button. When there is no dialectical interpretation, this is reported in the status bar, and the dialectical arguments remain unevaluated.

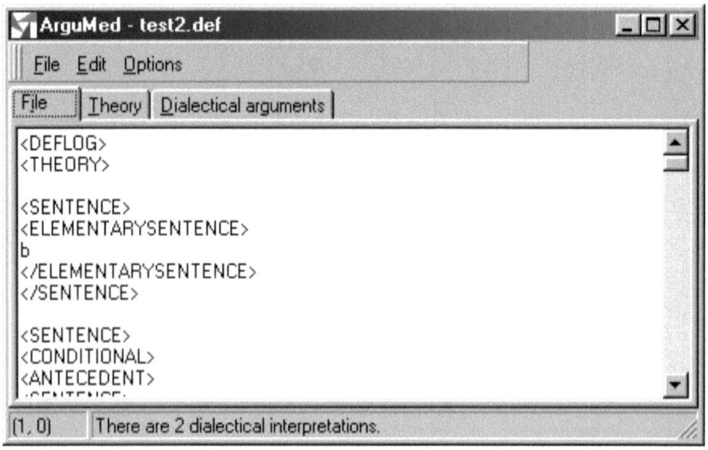

Figure 4.21: The file with the argumentative data

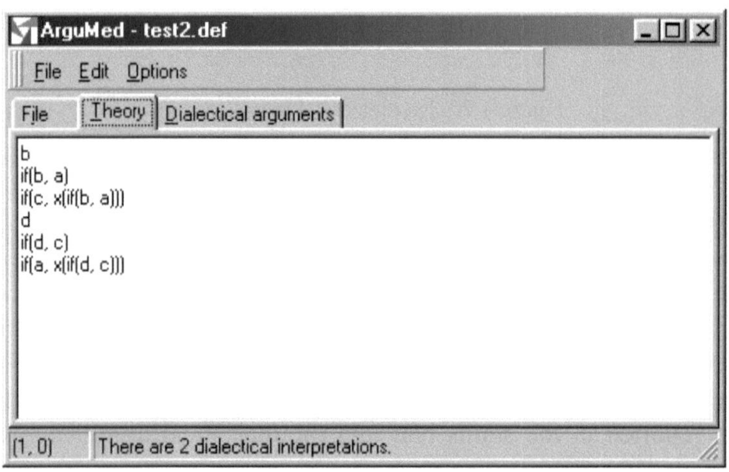

Figure 4.22: The prima facie justified assumptions

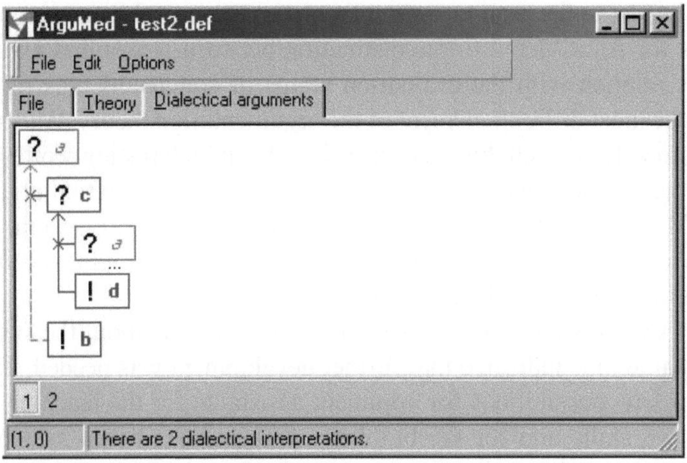

Figure 4.23: The dialectical arguments

4.4 USER EVALUATION

A group of eight law students (following a final year course in legal information technology) were asked to complete a test protocol concerning ARGUMED 3.0. The protocol was similar to the one used for ARGUMED 2.0 (see section 3.4). Again, initially little was explained, and the test persons were asked to discover the workings of the program for themselves. Before they were given explanations, the test persons were asked to interpret what they saw on screen. The test persons had to reproduce examples of arguments before they received information about the program's user interface.

A qualitative evaluation showed that the new interface of ARGUMED 3.0, using a mouse-sensitive screen was a success. The test persons reported few problems concerning the interaction with the system. Some suggested the possibility to drag statements to another location on the screen, to add a copy-paste function, and to make the colour scheme adaptable. The lack of a possibility to undo an action was reported. This was to be expected since a useful function of ARGUMED 2.0 was not available in ARGUMED 3.0: in ARGUMED 2.0, undoing and redoing was possible by moving back and forth in the line of argumentation. One test person wanted to be able to move the statements freely on the screen (as for instance in ARGUE!), perhaps with an optional sorting function.

With respect to the argumentation theory no great problems were reported. Just as for ArguMed 2.0, the distinction between issues and assumptions and its relation with the evaluation status of statements was reported as being the most difficult element of the argumentation theory. Warrants were understood fairly well, but were surprisingly and interestingly often avoided when the test persons were asked to represent a given textual argument in ArguMed 3.0. Just as in the evaluation of ArguMed 2.0, several test persons wanted a help function, such as a legend of the graphical elements, if only as a reminder of their meaning.

The test persons were, on the whole, enthusiastic about the system, but at the same time indicated that further development was needed. These test persons saw possibilities for argument assistants for the teaching of argumentative skills and for the building of knowledge-based systems. (The latter was probably induced in part by the fact that the test persons were following a course in legal information technology.) The graphical representation of arguments was assessed in different ways: some found it enlightening, others questioned the advantages over a textual representation. One test person was interested in the inclusion of legal knowledge in an argument assistant.

Chapter 5
A Comparison of Argument Assistants and Mediators

Chapter 5
A Comparison of Argument Assistants and Mediators

In this chapter, a number of argument assistants and mediators are discussed. The systems have been selected because of their graphical representation of argumentative data or because of the way in which they treat dialectical argumentation, i.e., argumentation with pros and cons.[1]

5.1 Belvedere

Belvedere is a system meant to stimulate critical discussion on scientific topics among middle-school and high-school students and to develop the skills required for such discussion. Belvedere allows the collaborative construction of so-called inquiry diagrams. An inquiry diagram is essentially a graphical representation of statements about the topic and their relations.

Several versions of Belvedere have been developed. Initially, Belvedere's statement types included principles, hypotheses, claims and unspecified statements. Statements could have several relations with one another: there were links meant to express support, explanation, causation, conjunction, conflict, justification and undercutting. In an inquiry diagram, the link types could be distinguished by their graphical representation and by their labels. Several of the link types could connect more than two statements, for instance to express support by a conjunction of statements. Some link types could also connect links. Suthers et al. (1995) report that the graphical ele-

[1] There are many other interesting systems in addition to the ones discussed here, for instance Nute's d-Prolog (1988), NATHAN by Loui and his students (1991-1993, <www.cs.wustl.edu/~loui/natnathan.text>), IACAS by Vreeswijk (1995), Pollock's OSCAR (1987, 1995), Tarski's World by Barwise and Etchemendy (2000), the systems by Span (2000) and Muntjewerff (2001), ABEL by Haenni, Kohlas and Lehmann (2001), Jaspars' logic animations (<turing.wins.uva.nl/~jaspars/animations/>), Reed and Walton's Araucaria (2001), <www.computing.dundee.ac.uk/staff/creed/research/araucaria.html>), Athena by Rolf and Magnusson (2002, <www.athenasoft.org>) and GeNIe (<www2.sis.pitt.edu/~genie/>). Tillers' work on MarshalPlan, a set of procedures and tools concerning reasoning with evidence in the law (<tillers.net/marshal.html>) is also of interest in this connection.

ments (used in what turned out to be the first version of Belvedere) are loosely based on Toulmin's (1958) scheme.

Later, the richness of statement and link types was abandoned (Suthers 1999). A reason for this was that it could occur that different reasonable choices were available, which led to unproductive discussion about the particular choice of category instead of about the topic. As a result, the number of options was limited in order to focus on those that were considered most important. For statements, only two types were distinguished, viz., data and hypothesis. Suthers (1999) reports that two link types remained, one intended to express the consistency of two statements, the other their inconsistency. Note that both are intended to express undirected relations, notwithstanding the fact that the link types are referred to as 'For links' and 'Against links' respectively, suggesting directedness. In the simplified Java applet version of Belvedere 3.0 (available at <lilt.ics.Hawaii.edu/lilt/software/belvedere/applet.html>), a third link type is used, called a 'non-link'. An example of a Belvedere screen showing an inquiry diagram is shown in figure 5.1.

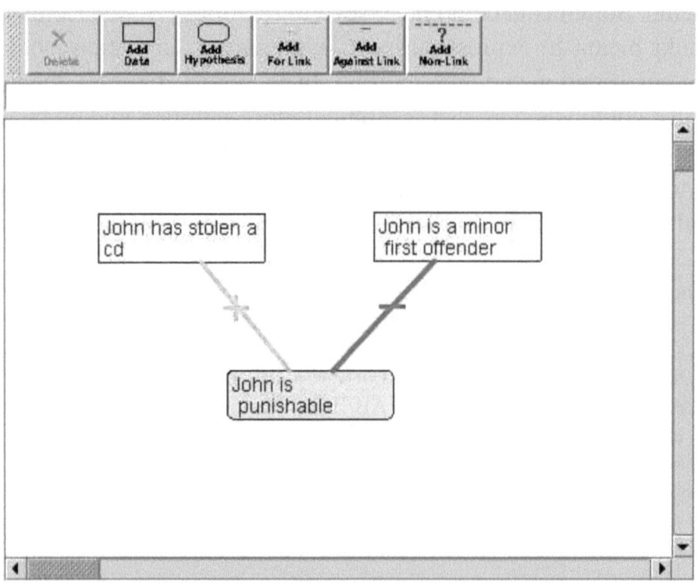

Figure 5.1: a Belvedere screen with an inquiry diagram

Inquiry diagrams are syntactic structures without an explicit semantics. An evaluative element is available in Belvedere's advisor (not in the applet version) (Paolucci et al. 1996, Toth et al. 1997). The advisor can give syntax-based hints telling students how to adapt the diagram. For instance, the advisor can ask the student whether there is support for an unsupported hypothesis. In later versions of Belvedere, an inquiry diagram could be compared with prespecified information about relevant statements, their mutual consistency and their evidential relations.

5.2 Convince Me

Convince Me[2] is an argumentation program supporting coherent reasoning, individually or in groups (Diehl, Ranney and Schank 2001, Ranney and Schank 1998, Schank 1995). It is based on the connectionist model ECHO, which simulates the principles of Thagard's (1992) theory of explanatory coherence.

Convince Me uses two statement types, viz., evidence and hypothesis, and two link types, viz., 'explain' and 'contradict'. It is a central assumption of the underlying theory of explanatory coherence that both link types are undirected: coherent beliefs are symmetrically supportive and incoherent beliefs are symmetrically conflicting. 'Explain' links can connect multiple statements to an explanandum. A simple network is shown in figure 5.2.

Note that both Convince Me and the later, simplified version of Belvedere (Suthers 1999) use very similar representations (cf., also figure 5.1) with two statement types and two undirected link types.

The networks in Convince Me can be evaluated by the system. Convince Me assigns each statement a numerical value (in the download version ranging from 1 to 9, in the publications from -1 to 1), using a constraint satisfaction algorithm. The computed statement values are the limit of a repeated process that takes statement values as input and returns new values. The process starts by taking certain default statement values as input. The process stops when the changes are sufficiently small or when a maximum number of steps have been reached. The computation of statement

[2] The program can be downloaded at <dewey.soe.berkeley.edu/~schank/convinceme/>.

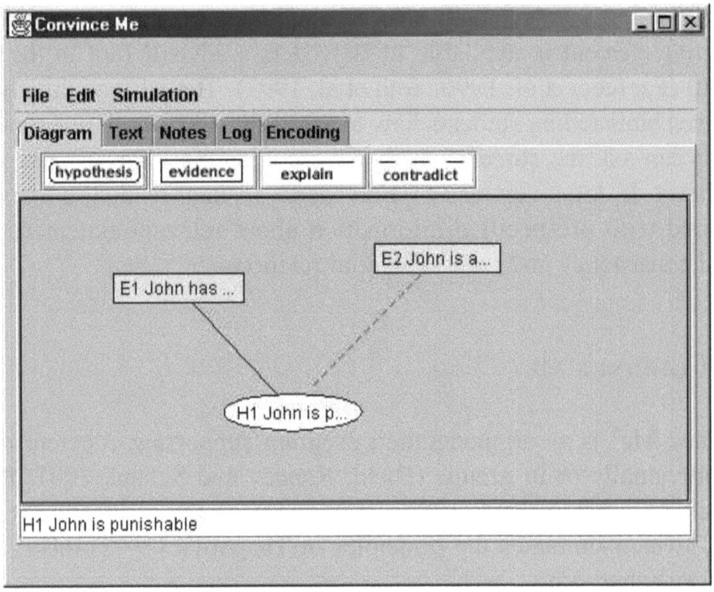

Figure 5.2: A network in Convince Me

values uses weighted excitatory and inhibitory links between statements that are computed from the network of explanation and contradiction links. In general, the set of excitatory and inhibitory links does not coincide with the set of explanation and contradiction links. For instance, when two evidence statements explain a hypothesis, each evidence statement excites the hypothesis, but they also excite each other. Further information on the algorithm is given in the reported sources.

The results of the example in figure 5.2 are shown in figure 5.3. The 'ECHO' column shows the computed values, the 'You' column shows the values as guessed by the user (or the default value 5). According to the log report, it has taken 75 rounds to compute these values. Evidence statement E1 (that John has stolen a cd) has a somewhat lower value than evidence statement E2 (that John is a minor first offender) since excitation and inhibition occur with different weights.[3] A network without explanation and

[3] By default, the excitation weight is set at .03 and the inhibition weight at .055. The user can change these values if required.

contradiction links returns the value 5 for hypotheses and 7.3 for evidence statements.

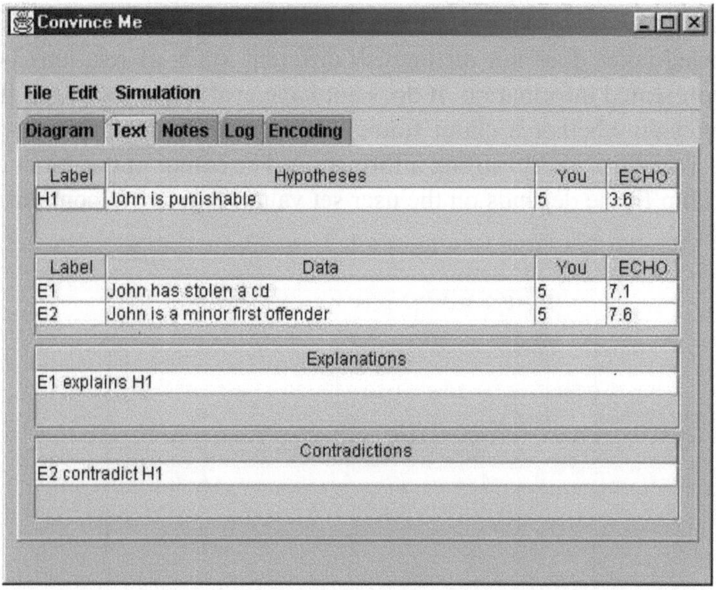

Figure 5.3: Results of statement evaluation by Convince Me

5.3 KIE's SenseMaker

SenseMaker is a tool for argument presentation (Bell 1997). It is part of a larger environment called KIE (the Knowledge Integration Environment).[4] More recently it has been included in WISE, a web-based science learning environment for use in schools.[5] Its functionality is very simple: it allows the organization of information in so-called claim frames. Claim frames are

[4] KIE's SenseMaker is not to be confused with the SenseMaker system that has been developed in the Stanford Digital Library Project (see <www-diglib.stanford.edu/diglib/pub/slides/sitevisit0497/sensemaker/>). The latter is an interface for information exploration across heterogeneous sources.

[5] Information on WISE, the Web-based Science Inquiry Environment, is available at <wise.berkeley.edu>. SenseMaker is not directly accessible, but it is possible to design a sample project in which SenseMaker can be approached.

titled rectangles that can contain other claim frames or evidence dots, i.e., web-links to pieces of evidence on the web. The idea is that the contents of a claim frame provide relevant evidence concerning the statement in the frame's title.

SenseMaker does not distinguish different kinds of relations between the represented information. It does not have evaluation tools, but the user can indicate whether a claim frame or an evidence dot expresses (very) weak, average or (very) strong information. The colour of the dot in the title of a claim frame depends on the user set value. Figure 5.4 contains an example.

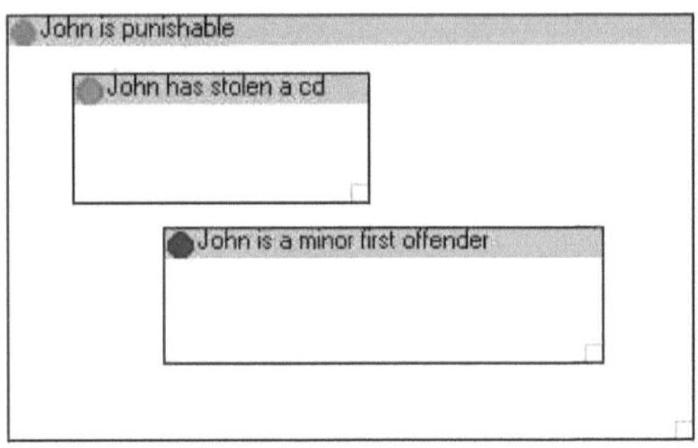

Figure 5.4: Claim frames in SenseMaker

5.4 REASON!ABLE

Reason!Able[6] is an argumentation program that is intended to improve critical thinking skills (Van Gelder 2001; see also <www.philosophy.unimelb.edu.au/reason/>). The program's interface is straightforward and easy to use, in particular because the program gives many contextual hints.

In Reason!Able, users can build argumentation diagrams. Argumentation diagrams basically consist of statements with reasons for them and objections against them. An example is shown in figure 5.5.

[6] A free trial version of the program is available at <www.goreason.com>.

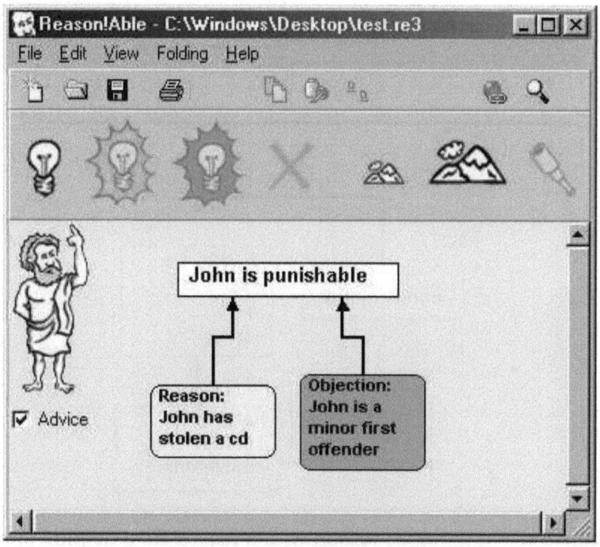

Figure 5.5: A Reason!Able sample screen

In Reason!Able, a reason or objection can consist of a group of statements. One of the statements that form a reason or objection is called the main premise of the reason or objection, the others are referred to as helping premises. Figure 5.6 shows an example. The statement that John is a thief is the main claim of a reason, and the statement that if John is a thief, then he is punishable, is a helping premise.[7] In general, any statement (and not only conditionals) can be added as helping premises. The helping premise itself is supported by the reason that thieves are punishable.

An interesting feature of Reason!Able's interface is that composite reasons can be folded and unfolded: when a composite reason is folded, only the main premise of the reason is visible. Folding composite reasons can help in keeping track of the most relevant statements. In figure 5.7 the composite reason of figure 5.6 is shown in its folded state. A counterintuitive side-effect is that reasons for helping premises appear as reasons for the main premise when a composite reason is folded. For instance, in the figure, the statement that thieves are punishable incorrectly appears as a reason for the statement that John is a thief.

[7] Reason!Able has a template form for *Modus ponens* arguments. In the template, typing the main premise P of a reason for Q results in the generation of the helping premise IF P THEN Q.

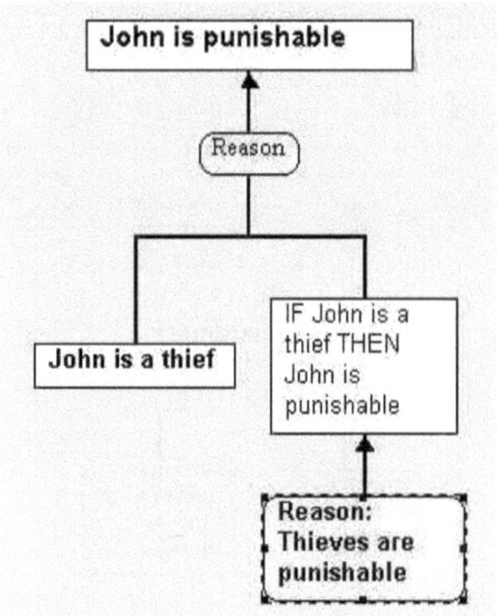

Figure 5.6: An unfolded reason with a reason for a helping premise

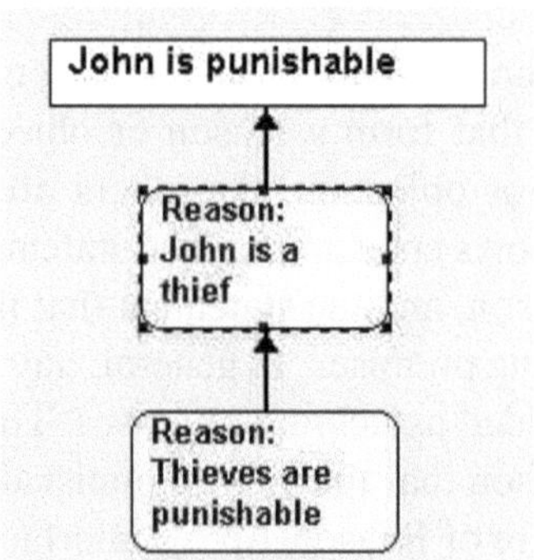

Figure 5.7: After folding, a reason for a helping premise looks like a reason for the main premise

When an argument has been built, Reason!Able can guide the user through an evaluation process. Evaluation starts with statements at the bottom of an argument, that have no reasons or objections. The user can pick one of six values for the main conclusion and the premises composing reasons and objections: not evaluated, definitely false, probably false, no verdict, probably true, definitely true. For reasons, the user can select one of five values: not evaluated, no support, weak support, strong support, conclusive support. For objections, the user can select from a similar range of degrees of opposition. The statements at the bottom, i.e., those without reasons and objections, can be given one of a series of grounds: common knowledge, personal knowledge, expert opinion, testimony, considered plausibility, necessary truth, no grounds apply or not evaluated.

The evaluation of statements, reasons and objections is left entirely to the user, and is not constrained by the system. Setting a ground for a statement does give rise to the default evaluation 'probably true' (except for the grounds 'no grounds apply' and 'not evaluated' which give rise to the value 'no verdict' and 'not evaluated', respectively). The default evaluations can be adapted at will, however. For instance, it is possible to evaluate a main conclusion as definitely false, while it only has a reason that is evaluated as providing conclusive support. Reason!Able's help file does provide guidelines to be followed, such as a statement with a single conclusive reason should be evaluated as definitely true.

An important issue is how Reason!Able treats Pollock-style undercutters. This is discussed in Reason!Able's help file, under the topic objections to inferences. The answer is that in Reason!Able an objection to an inference should be represented as an objection to a helping premise. An example is shown in figure 5.8. Note that folding the reason has the counterintuitive effect that the objection to the helping premise looks like an objection to the main premise (cf. the analogous effect for reasons for helping premises; figures 5.6 and 5.7).

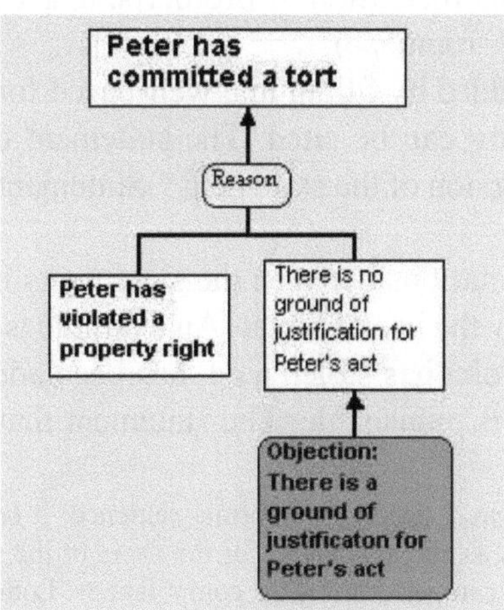

Figure 5.8: An 'undercutter' in Reason!Able

Toulmin-style warrants are not explicitly dealt with in Reason!Able's help file, but from the examples it seems that a warrant is considered as a helping premise. Figure 5.9 shows an example of a warrant as a helping premise, and its backing.

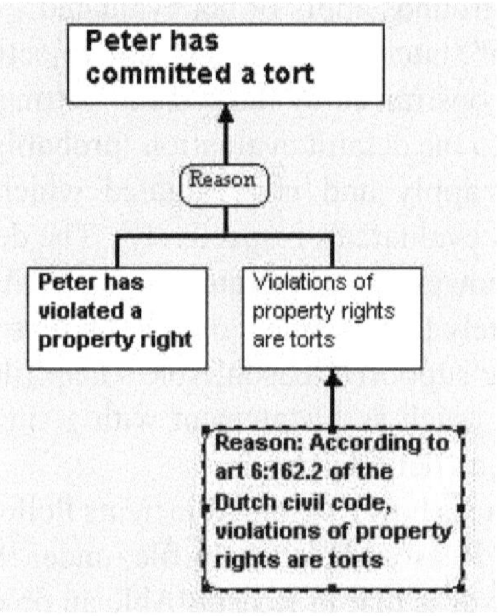

Figure 5.9: A 'warrant' and its backing in Reason!Able

5.5 Room 5

Room 5 (Loui et al. 1997) is presented as a testbed for public interactive semi-formal legal argumentation. A prototype is available on the web (see <www.cs.wustl.edu/~room5/>).

Statements are added by filling in a web-based form. When a statement is added, an authority can be cited. The statement can also be annotated with a formalized version of the statement.[8] Statements can be attacked and supported.

In Room 5, the relations between the statements in an argument are visually represented by the use of boxes. An example is shown in figure 5.10. The statement that John has stolen a cd, has been added as support for the statement that John is punishable. The statement that John is a minor first

[8] Occasionally, Room 5 generates a formal sentence. It seems that the formal sentences are mainly meant as an explanation for the users of the system and not as expressions on which Room 5 can perform logical computations. Loui et al. (1997) do not fully explain the formalism and its role.

offender has been added as an attack against John's punishability. Each statement is shown inside a box. A statement's support occurs in boxes inside the statement's box. Attacking statements are shown in a box to the right of the statement's box.

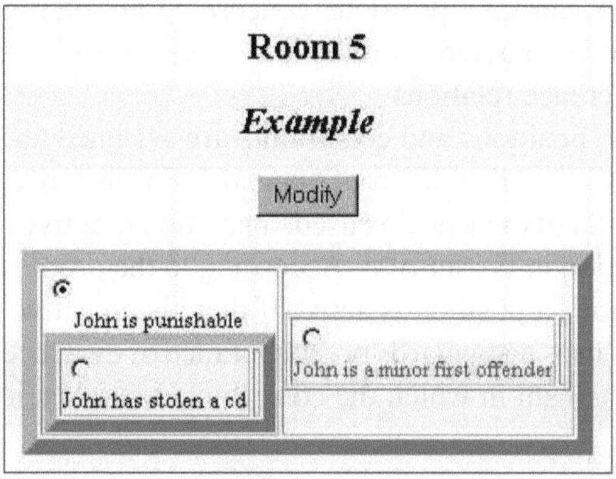

Figure 5.10: The box representation of arguments in Room 5

Room 5's box representation of arguments has been developed in order to avoid the 'pointer spaghetti' that can result from an arrow representation.[9]

5.6 ZENO AND HERMES

The Zeno project studies and implements systems that support and mediate online discussions (Gordon et al. 2001; see also <zeno.fhg.de>). Zeno uses Rittel's IBIS (Rittel and Webber 1973) as its underlying argumentation model. Initially, it was planned to use an extended version of IBIS as the core of Zeno (viz., the argumentation framework described in Gordon and Karacapilidis 1997), but this was not implemented (Gordon et al. 1999). There are plans to build a version of Zeno with an adaptable argumentation framework and discourse model.

Karacapilidis and Papadias (2001) have implemented the Hermes system that uses a variant of Gordon and Karacapilidis's (1997) Zeno frame-

[9] Loui et al. (1997, p. 209) claim that it 'can be especially confusing when arrows have both attack and support semantics'. The confusion arising in their Toulmin-like example (n. viii) indeed results from the fact that the same type of arrow is used for attack and for support. Confusion of this kind does not occur when different types of arrows are used.

work as its underlying argumentation model. The basic elements are issues, alternatives, positions and constraints. An issue (labelled 'i' in the example screen in figure 5.11) is a decision that is to be made or a goal that is to be achieved. Users can propose alternatives (labelled 'a') that can deal with the issue. Users can take positions concerning an alternative (or another position), either for or against it (labelled '+' and '–'). Constraints are meant to express preference relations.

Alternatives, positions and constraints are assigned an activation label, determined by the applicable proof standard. For instance, when the proof standard 'scintilla of evidence' is used, a position is active if there is at least one active position in favour of it. According to the proof standard 'beyond reasonable doubt', a position is active if there is no active position against it. Hermes also uses a standard 'preponderance of evidence' that involves a weighting mechanism in which the constraints are taken into account.

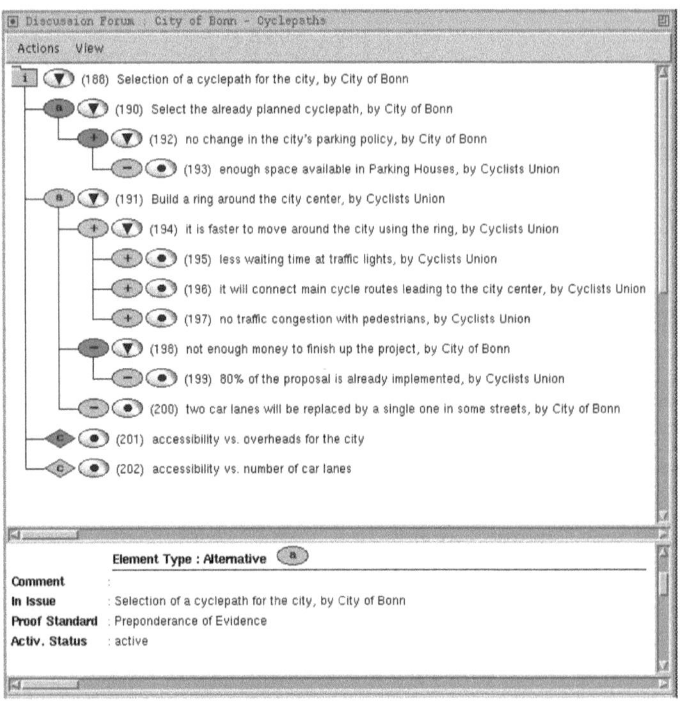

Figure 5.11: A sample screen of the Hermes system[10]

[10] The screen is taken from Hermes' user manual at <www-sop.inria.fr/aid/hermes/>.

5.7 Overview and Comparison

In table 5.1, an overview is given of the argumentation theories of the systems discussed in this chapter. It is indicated what types of statements are used, which elements can be used for the structuring of the argumentative information, whether warrants are handled or not, and whether it is possible to use undercutters in argumentation.

System	**Statement types**	**Structuring elements**	**Warrants**	**Undercutters**
Belvedere	data and hypothesis	for and against links, non-links (all undirected)	no	no
Convince Me	evidence and hypothesis	explain and contradiction links (undirected)	no	no
KIE's SenseMaker	claim frames and evidence dots	frames	no	no
Reason!Able	statements, reasons, objections, grounds	reason and objection links	in terms of helping premises	in terms of helping premises
Room 5	statements	horizontally and vertically arranged boxes	authority annotations	no
Zeno and Hermes	issues, alternatives, positions (for and against), constraints	tree hierarchy	no	no
ARGUE!	statements	reason links, defeaters	no	in terms of defeaters
ARGUMED 2.0	assumptions and issues	reason and undercutter links	yes (including undercutter warrants)	yes
ARGUMED 3.0	assumptions and issues	support and attack links	yes	yes

Table 5.1: Overview of the systems' argumentation theories

It turns out that in most programs considered, at least two types of statement are distinguished, roughly corresponding to the distinction between assumptions and issues in ArguMed.

In several systems in the table both support and attack links between statements can be used. Interestingly, some systems (Convince Me and Belvedere) use undirected link types.

Warrants and undercutters are not or are hardly dealt with. One reason might be that warrants and undercutters are not as obviously needed in argumentation as support and attack. In Reason!Able, warrants and undercutters can be dealt with by the use of helping premises. However, this conceals the special character of warrants and undercutters, namely as reasons for and against the connections between statements. ArguMed 3.0 shows that that character can be brought to the fore in a straightforward way.

Table 5.2 provides an overview of the functionality and interface of the discussed systems. It is indicated how argumentation can be evaluated, how argumentative data are visualized and how the user interacts with the system.

Several systems allow some kind of evaluation of the argumentative data. In Reason!Able the evaluation can be carried out by the user, unconstrained by the system. In Zeno and Hermes, and the two ArguMed systems, the system performs the evaluation itself. Argue! also carries out an automatic evaluation, but its algorithm is step by step: the user determines when the system makes the next evaluative step.

There is one major dichotomy in the style of visualization of the argumentative data: the boxes-and-links style, that uses boxes, lines and arrows (used by most systems), and the nested-boxes style, in which the argument hierarchy is indicated by boxes inside boxes (used by KIE's SenseMaker and Room 5). Well-designed empirical research might be able to establish that one style leads to argument representations that are easier to read for a user than the other. From a design perspective the boxes-and-links style seems to allow more variation than the nested-boxes style, thus allowing more fruitful representations.

In some systems, the argumentative data is arranged by the system, in others by the user. Both have advantages and disadvantages. An advantage of arrangement by the system is that the information is consistently ordered. However, adding new information can lead to unexpected rearrange-

System	**Evaluation**	**Visualization**	**Interaction**
Belvedere	no	boxes and links arranged by user	template form
Convince Me	numerical constraint satisfaction algorithm	boxes and links arranged by user	template form
KIE's SenseMaker	no	nested boxes arranged by user	template form
Reason!Able	unconstrained user input	boxes and links arranged by system	mouse-sensitive screen (move-based)
Room 5	no	nested boxes arranged by system	template form
Zeno and Hermes	algorithm based on proof standards	tree arranged by system	template form
ARGUE!	defeasible logic algorithm (stepwise)	boxes and links arranged by user	mouse-sensitive screen (structure-based)
ARGUMED 2.0	defeasible logic algorithm	boxes and links arranged by system	template form
ARGUMED 3.0	defeasible logic algorithm	boxes and links arranged by system	mouse-sensitive screen (move-based)

Table 5.2: Overview of the systems' functionality and interface

ments, in the sense that sentences can jump to a very different location on the screen. An advantage of arrangement by the user is the feeling of control perceived by the user: no information can become lost. Whether that advantage outweighs the disadvantage of a less consistent arrangement probably depends on the situation. It can be expected that a flexible system that allows both arrangement by the system and by the user maximizes user satisfaction.

Two interaction types can be distinguished: interaction using template forms, i.e., forms that can be filled in by the user, and interaction using a mouse-sensitive screen. Template forms are generally user-friendly. However, a drawback of templates is that it is not always easy for users to make the connection between what happens on screen and the data they fill in on the template. A mouse-sensitive screen has an obvious advantage in this respect: the user modifies the data onscreen by directly interacting with it.

Interaction using a mouse-sensitive screen can be designed in two ways: with a focus on the graphical structures or on the argumentation moves. For instance, the interaction of the ARGUE! system focuses on the graphical structures. The user can 'draw' statement boxes, arrows and defeater directly on the screen. Clicking a button determines the graphical mode, i.e., whether a statements box, an arrow or a defeater is drawn. Instead, ARGUMED 3.0 focuses on the argumentation moves, such as adding a statement or providing support. For instance, when the user clicks a statement, he can directly provide support for it. As a result, working with ARGUE! is a very different experience from working with ARGUMED 3.0. The latter gives a more natural feeling than the former. An explanation for this effect can be that interaction focusing on argumentation moves is closer to what the user is doing than interaction focusing on the graphical elements: he is not drawing graphical representations, but engaging in argumentation. This suggests that interaction should be designed focusing on argumentation moves and not on graphical elements.

Chapter 6
Theories of Defeasible Argumentation

Chapter 6
Theories of Defeasible Argumentation

The average arguer will admit that for most of his arguments it is conceivable that they are successfully attacked. Many will consider it possible that additional information can lead to the retraction of conclusions that appeared to be justified. In other words, arguments are commonly taken to be defeasible.

The topic of defeasible argumentation (cf., also section 1.2) has turned out to be notoriously difficult from a theoretical point of view. A huge amount of research effort has been spent on defeasible argumentation, especially in the field of artificial intelligence (where much of the relevant work goes by the label nonmonotonic logic; cf., the 1994 handbook by Gabbay et al.) and its subfield AI & law (cf., Prakken 1993, 1997; Hage 1997; the special issue of *Artificial Intelligence and Law*, 2000, Nos. 2-3). Since much of this work is highly technical in nature, the insights have not been well disseminated into the field of argumentation theory. Luckily there is a tendency of cross-fertilization, especially by the connection of defeasible argumentation with argumentative dialogues, which for a long time have been central in argumentation-theoretic approaches (cf., the pragmadialectical approach of Van Eemeren and Grootendorst 1981, 1987, and Walton's new dialectic 1998; see also Walton and Krabbe 1995). Hart introduced the term 'defeasibility' in the 1940s (cf., Loui 1995). Many insights on defeasible argumentation that continue to inspire researchers can be found in the work of Toulmin (1958) and Rescher (1977). Good recent overviews are Prakken and Vreeswijk's (2002) and Chesñevar et al.'s (2000).

In this chapter, the argumentation theories underlying the argument assistants presented in this book are briefly compared to a selection of existing theories of defeasible argumentation. Knowledge of those theories is assumed. The chapter expands discussions by Verheij (1999a, 2000a). Each subsection starts with a brief overview of a theory of defeasible argumentation, and then discusses how it treats arguing with pros and cons, arguing with warrants, argument evaluation and theory construction (cf. the four points of focus listed in section 1.2).

6.1 Toulmin's Argument Scheme[1]

In his book 'The Uses of Argument', Stephen Toulmin (1958) argued that arguments need to be analyzed using a richer format than the traditional one of formal logic in which only premises and conclusions are distinguished. He proposed a scheme that, next to *data* and *claim*, distinguishes between *warrant*, *backing*, *rebuttal* and *qualifier*.

As an illustration, Toulmin discussed the claim that Harry is a British subject. The claim can be supported by the datum that Harry was born in Bermuda. That there is a connection at all between the datum and claim is expressed by the warrant that a man born in Bermuda will generally be a British subject. In its turn, the warrant can be supported by the backing that there are certain statutes and other legal provisions to that effect. The warrant does not have total justifying force, so the claim that Harry is a British subject must be qualified: it presumably follows. In addition to this, there are possible rebuttals, for instance when both his parents were aliens or he has become a naturalized American.

Schematically, the result is as follows (Toulmin 1958, p. 105):

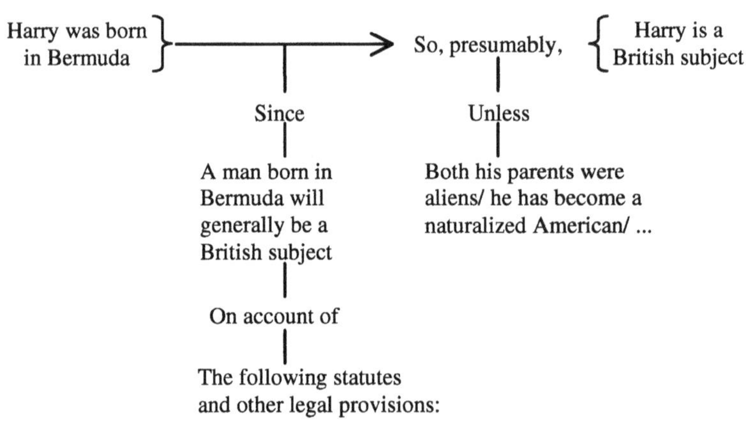

Toulmin's argument scheme has had a continuing influence on argumentation researchers (cf., e.g., Van Eemeren et al. 1996, pp. 129-160; Bench-Capon 1997). Its general form is thus (Toulmin 1958, p. 104):

[1] The present section contains material from Verheij (1999a, 2001a).

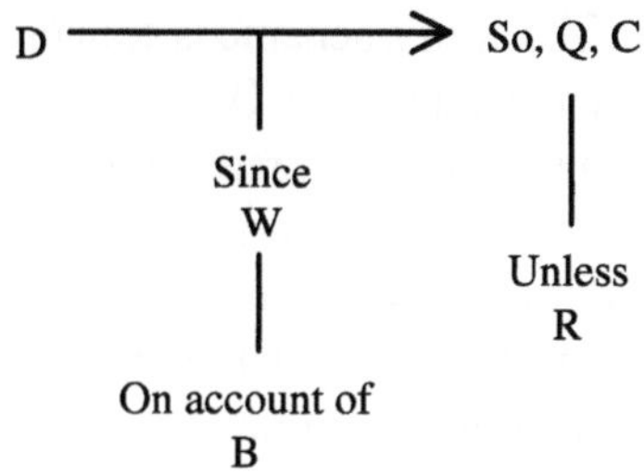

D for *Datum*
Q for *Qualifier*
C for *Claim*

W for *Warrant*
B for *Backing*
R for *Rebuttal*

The Datum consists of certain facts that support the Claim. The Warrant is an inference licence according to which the Datum supports the Claim, while the Backing, in its turn, provides support for the Warrant. A Rebuttal provides conditions of exception for the argument, and the Qualifier can express a degree of force that the Datum gives to the Claim by the Warrant.

What did Toulmin say about our four argumentation-theoretic points of focus? Toulmin's scheme addresses two of them: arguing with pros and cons and arguing with warrants. The other two – argument evaluation and theory construction – fall outside the scope of Toulmin's (1958) work.

6.1.1 **Arguing with pros and cons**

The introduction of the element of rebuttal in his scheme is a clear recognition that arguing not only involves pros, but also cons. Toulmin hardly elaborates on the nature of rebuttals. On the one hand, he said that rebuttals can 'indicate circumstances in which the general authority of the warrant would have to be set aside' (p. 101). But rebuttals can also be (and for Toulmin apparently equivalently) 'exceptional circumstances which might be capable of defeating or rebutting the warranted conclusion' (p. 101). It seems that for Toulmin both concepts can go by the name of rebuttal. However, the former phrasing makes rebuttals a kind of undercutting reason (cf., Pollock 1987),[2] while the latter phrasing makes them reasons against the conclusion. These are different concepts. Let us look at both interpretations of rebuttals.

[2] He speaks of undercutting defeaters and not of undercutting reasons.

When the rebuttal R in Toulmin's scheme is conceived of as a reason against a claim C (for convenience a qualifier Q is omitted here), there is a conflict of reasons: there is at the same time a reason for C, viz., the datum D, and a reason against it, viz., R. In one natural interpretation of such a situation, the rebuttal is a reason for the negation of C. As a result, in order to determine whether or not C follows, it must somehow be determined which of the two reasons is most important: does one outweigh the other, does one have priority? It can then of course be the case that R is the better reason, and therefore that C does not follow, while its negation does.

The analysis is different when the rebuttal R is an undercutting reason. Then the rebuttal C is a reason against D's being a reason for C. As a result, R blocks the connection between D and C, but otherwise is not relevant as a reason for or against C. When R is an undercutting reason, there is no conflict of reasons concerning the claim C. When R is effective, all that follows is that D cannot justify C. As a result, C does not follow (and neither does its negation).

6.1.2 Arguing with warrants

Arguing with warrants lies at the heart of Toulmin's (1958) work. One of his main points is that the warrants of arguments (in the sense of generic inference licenses) can be at issue and that their backings can differ from domain to domain. Toulmin's warrants are answers to the question why datum and claim are connected, or – as Toulmin put it – to the question 'How do you get there?' (p. 97f.). Interestingly, however, his warrants only concern the connection between the datum and the claim. Surprisingly, he did not discuss the similar need for a warrant of the role of the rebuttal. Still it is clear that it can be at issue whether some rebuttal is actually a reason against the claim. Similarly, it can be at issue whether a rebuttal is an undercutting reason. For instance, in Dutch law, the lack of culpability cannot exclude the fact that one has committed a tort. When the lack of culpability is nevertheless used as a counterargument, it is the 'rebuttal warrant' that needs to be argued against. Such 'rebuttal warrants' provide an answer to the question 'How does that get us away from there?' Just as a claim is not supported by any statement whatsoever, it is not the case that any statement can serve as a rebuttal. Just as a warrant is needed to show that a statement supports a claim, a warrant is needed to show that a statement rebuts it.

In other words, Toulmin only distinguished support warrants, whereas there also is a need for attack warrants. In the law, the need for both support warrants and attack warrants becomes obvious when one realizes that not only rules need backing, e.g., by citing a statutory article, but also exceptions. For instance, Article 6:162.2 Dutch civil code (which says that – amongst other things – violations of property rights are torts unless there is a ground of justification) provides a backing for a support warrant, viz., that violations of property rights are torts, and a backing for an attack warrant, viz., that grounds of justification can result in a violation of a property right not being a tort.

6.1.3 **Argument evaluation**

Toulmin did not discuss argument evaluation. He only discussed the *structure* of arguments (in terms of the roles of the different kinds of elements of arguments). In other words, he did not provide an analogue of logical *validity* as an evaluation criterion for arguments. Of course this was also not his focus.

A discussion as to why he did not pay attention to argument evaluation would have been interesting. Perhaps Toulmin did not believe that evaluation could make sense for his extended view on argument structure.

Rebuttals have an obvious effect on the evaluation of an argument however. Clearly, if there (actually) is a rebuttal, then an argument should be evaluated differently than if there is no rebuttal. Using Toulmin's example above, it depends on the fact whether Harry's parents were aliens, whether the datum that Harry was born in Bermuda justifies the claim that he is a British subject. Assuming that Harry's parents were aliens, the datum does *not* justify the claim, while assuming that they were not aliens, the datum will normally justify the claim (unless there is another rebuttal, such as the fact that Harry has become a naturalized American). As said, perhaps Toulmin did not believe that there was an evaluation criterion analogous to logical validity. Recent work on the evaluation of defeasible argumentation has shown otherwise. Verheij (2001a) applies the argumentation theory underlying ArguMed 3.0 (chapter 4) to Toulmin's scheme and provides a way to evaluate arguments based on the scheme.

6.1.4 Theory construction

Toulmin did not discuss theory construction. This is not surprising since he did not put his argumentation theory in a procedural context.

6.2 Reiter's Logic for Default Reasoning

Next, Reiter's (1980, 1987) logic for default reasoning deserves discussion, since it can be considered as a theory of defeasible argumentation *avant la lettre*.

In Reiter's formalism, a default is an expression $\alpha : M\beta_1, ..., M\beta_m / \gamma$, where α, $\beta_1, ..., \beta_m$, and γ are first-order sentences. The sentence α is the default's prerequisite, the sentences β_i are its justification and the sentence γ its consequent. Intuitively, a default's consequent follows when its prerequisite holds and when its justifications can consistently be assumed. Reiter formally elaborates this intuition in his definition of extensions of default theories.

A general difference between Reiter's default logic and the argumentation theories underlying the systems presented in this book is that the former uses a first-order language with variables and quantifiers, whereas the languages of the latter only use sentence connectives.

Of our four argumentation-theoretic points of focus, Reiter's work is especially relevant for arguing with pros and cons and argument evaluation.

6.2.1 Arguing with pros and cons

Reiter's default logic has natural connections with arguing with pros and cons. One way of representing pros and cons in default logic is by using so-called normal defaults, i.e., defaults that only have the default's consequent as justification. For instance, assume that α is a reason for γ and β a reason against it. Then the normal defaults $\alpha : M\gamma / \gamma$ and $\beta : M\neg\gamma / \neg\gamma$ (where $\neg$ denotes standard negation) can be used as a representation. According to Reiter's definitions the situation is ambiguous: there are two extensions, given α and β and the two defaults. In either extension only one of the defaults is applied. One extension contains γ by the application of the first default, the other $\neg\gamma$ by the application of the second. In a sense either extension represents the situation that one reason is stronger than the other. A sceptical reasoner will accept neither γ nor $\neg\gamma$ since neither is in both extensions, a credulous reasoner will accept both since both are in some extension.

At the time, Reiter knew of 'no naturally occurring default which cannot be represented in this [normal, BV] form' (1987, p. 75). Already Reiter and Criscuolo (1981, 1987) noted that normal defaults do not suffice from a representational point of view. So-called semi-normal defaults, i.e., defaults that have their consequent as one of their justifications are also needed. Semi-normal defaults are for instance required in order to represent undercutting reasons (in Pollock's 1987 sense). For instance, if γ is an undercutting reason blocking α as a reason for β, this can be represented as $\alpha : M\beta, M\neg\gamma / \beta$. Given this default and α, but not γ, there is one extension containing β. The default is applied since its justifications β and $\neg\gamma$ can both be consistently assumed. Given the default and both α and γ, there is also one extension, but it does not contain β. The default is not applied since its justifications $\neg\gamma$ cannot be applied. A drawback of the representation is that it does not represent the reason and the undercutter separately: the relation between α, β and γ must be represented in one single default.

Prakken (1993, 1997) extensively discusses the representational possibilities of Reiter's default logic in the context of the law. (See also chapter 4 of Verheij 1996a.)

6.2.2 Arguing with warrants

Arguing with warrants is not easily representable in Reiter's default logic. The reason for this is that defaults – which are the natural candidate for the representation of warrants – cannot be at issue. Defaults can only be assumed, but they cannot follow from other assumptions. As a result, common examples involving the backing of a warrant, e.g., in a legal setting by providing a statutory article in which a legal rule is laid down, do not have a natural representation in Reiter's default logic.

6.2.3 Argument evaluation

Since Reiter's formalism does not have an explicit notion of argument, argument evaluation is not directly addressed. However, an important role of argument evaluation is to determine which conclusions follow from given assumptions. In Reiter's default logic, the notion of extensions of default theories is used for this role: extensions specify sets of consequences of a default theory.

A notorious property of extensions is that default theories do not always have a unique extension. It is also possible that there is no extension or that there are several.

One reaction to the non-uniqueness of extensions has been to define a unique set of consequences of a default theory in terms of its extensions. A credulous and a sceptical set of consequences can be defined by taking the union or the intersection of the set of extensions of a default theory. A drawback of the credulous and the sceptical approach is that neither the union nor the intersection of the set of extensions are in general themselves extensions. Whereas an extension has a strong internal coherence, in which it is entirely clear why some defaults have been applied and others have not, this is generally not the case in the union or intersection of all extensions. In the light of this, it seems to be more suitable to consider each extension of a default theory (if existing) as one of perhaps several sets of consequences of the default theory. Perhaps it is simply to be admitted that the situation in standard logic – where it makes perfect sense to focus on the unique set of consequences – differs fundamentally from that in defeasible logic – where it makes perfect sense that some theories do not have an extension or do not have a unique one.

6.2.4 **Theory construction**

The topic of theory construction is not addressed by Reiter's default logic (1980, 1987) since the theory is not presented in a procedural context (although Reiter does pay some attention to belief revision).

6.3 Pollock's Rebutting and Undercutting Defeaters

Pollock's (1987, 1995) theory of defeasible reasoning has been very influential. He has presented his theory in the context of making an intelligent agent (as the subtitle of his 1995 book shows: 'A blueprint for how to build a person'). His work has a strong philosophical orientation. However, since

Pollock intends to build a computer program and actually did so in his OSCAR architecture (see <www.u.arizona.edu/~pollock/oscar.html>), his theorizing always takes place with operational considerations in mind. In his 1995 book, he not only discusses the structure of defeasible reasoning, but also epistemic cognition, and the making of plans. Pollock's 1995 book is exemplary in the breadth of topics addressed and in the thorough philosophical discussion.

Pollock's work addresses three of the argumentation-theoretic points of focus of the present research: arguing with pros and cons, argument evaluation and theory construction. Arguing with warrants seems to fall outside Pollock's scope.

6.3.1 **Arguing with pros and cons**

Perhaps the most influential aspect of Pollock's work is his distinction between rebutting and undercutting defeaters:

> 'There are two importantly different kinds of defeaters. Where *P* is a prima facie reason for *Q*, *R* is a *rebutting defeater* iff *R* is a reason for denying *Q*. [...] Undercutting defeaters attack the connection between the reason and the conclusion rather than attacking the conclusion directly.'
>
> (Pollock 1995, p. 40-41; see also p. 85-86)

According to Pollock, rebutting defeaters as they actually occur always have associated undercutting defeaters.

Pollock's notion of inference graphs is related to the dialectical arguments of ArguMed. However, Pollock does not construct his graphs from statements, but from so-called sequents, i.e., pairs of premises and conclusions.[3]

Pollock chooses to treat rebutting and undercutting defeaters as separate concepts, even though they seem to be instances of some common abstract concept of defeaters. Pollock's definition of the effect of undercutting and rebutting defeaters on nodes in an inference graph already points in this direction (1995, p. 93): there the different effects of rebutting and undercutting are combined into a single effect, namely defeat.

---

[3] A sequent is a pair (S, φ), where S is a set of sentences and φ is a sentence. A sequent (S,φ) expresses that j follows from S.

It therefore seems worthwhile to look for a concept of defeater that comprises both rebutting and undercutting defeaters. Verheij's CUMULA (1996a, chapter 5) provides an attempt in this direction, leading to other kinds of defeaters (cf., section 6.7). Another approach unifying kinds of defeaters is the argumentation theory underlying ARGUMED 3.0. The key idea is to explicitly express the defeat of statements, including the defeat of conditional statements. When R undercuts P as a reason for Q, the relation between the statements can be expressed as $R \leadsto \times(P \leadsto Q)$, where $\times$ expresses defeat (cf., section 4.1.4 on DEFLOG). Interestingly, Pollock discusses expressions of the form 'P wouldn't be true unless Q were true', denoted as $\ulcorner P >> Q \urcorner$, and then treats undercutting defeaters as reasons for denying such $\ulcorner P >> Q \urcorner$, but does not make the generalizing (and thereby simplifying) step of introducing an expression for the defeat of a statement.

Pollock discusses the use of numerical weights that measure the strengths of reasons. This topic is not addressed in the research presented here.

6.3.2 **Arguing with warrants**

Pollock does not address arguing with warrants that are at issue. His discussion of rules of inference (Pollock 1995, p. 89-90) suggests that he considers warrants (in Toulmin's 1958 sense of generic inference licences) as given, undisputed assumptions. The examples he gives are directly inspired by rules of natural deduction of standard logic (see, e.g., Van Dalen 1983 or Gamut 1991), and for most purposes these rules can indeed remain undisputed. However, even these rules can occasionally be the topic of discussion: in particular the logical rules of negation and the material conditional have led to a great deal of debate by philosophers of logic and mathematics.

In a broader perspective on warrants they can be put at issue. For instance, whether a particular rule is a rule of law is often the subject of discussion.

As said, Pollock discusses expressions of the form 'P wouldn't be true unless Q were true'. These expressions seem to be related to instances of warrants. However, these expressions are apparently only used for the characterization of undercutting defeaters: a defeater is a reason denying such an expression. It is not clear whether it is Pollock's intention to allow giving reasons for these expressions.

6.3.3 **Argument evaluation**

Pollock's inference graphs have already been mentioned. They are related to the dialectical arguments of ArguMed. Pollock's inference graphs consist of nodes that can represent premises and conclusions,[4] support-links that represent an inference from one node to the next, and defeaters that represent the blocking of an inference. Note that in Pollock's theory, defeaters can block an inference to a node, and cannot directly attack nodes. When a node is defeated this actually means that inferring the node is blocked. This assumes a two-layered view on defeasible reasoning (cf., also Prakken 1997 on argumentation layers): in the first layer there are chains of inference that connect statements (or sequents), and in the second there are defeat relations that can block the inferences in the first. This two-layered nature is also reflected in Pollock's discussion of a monotonic reasoner, on top of which a defeasible reasoner is built (cf., chapter 4 of Pollock 1995).[5]

This two-layered nature is in contrast with the argumentation theory of ArguMed. In ArguMed, support and attack occur on the same level: both support and attack connect statements, and it is not the inferences that are defeated, but the statements themselves. What is treated as the defeat of an inference in Pollock's theory, is treated as the defeat of a conditional statement in the theory underlying ArguMed. In ArguMed, defeat is expressible in the logical language (in terms of dialectical negation).

Inference graphs are evaluated by computing the defeat status of their nodes. Some of the underlying intuitions are similar to the evaluation of ArguMed's dialectical arguments. For instance, nodes that are not attacked and that have no attacked ancestors (so-called D-initial nodes) are undefeated. Pollock distinguishes between undefeated and defeated nodes. Nodes can be defeated outright or they can be provisionally defeated. Pollock discusses a series of possible definitions (1995, p. 110, 114, 118, 120-124). He formulates several constraints for the evaluation function, and then adapts them on a number of occasions. For instance, he changes the definition after arguing that a self-defeating node should be defeated outright rather than just provisionally (p. 115).

---

4 As said, nodes are sequents. See note 3.

5 It can be argued that Pollock's theory actually consists of three layers. The first consisting of sequents (see note 3), the second of inferences from one sequent to the next, and the third of defeaters of such inferences.

Perhaps as a consequence of Pollock's strategy of gradually changing his definitions by studying examples, the resulting evaluation function is not very transparent. The changes are however guided by problems that have also been encountered elsewhere in the relevant research literature. Pollock makes many interesting observations and shows different kinds of approaches to address the phenomena he discusses.

Pollock takes the possibility into account that the inference graph determined by a given input is not completely available at the start of reasoning, but needs to be gradually computed. And since the reasoning involves defeasible inferences, a node's evaluation can change when the inference graph is extended.

As a result Pollock discusses two kinds of limit situations of the evaluation of the nodes in an inference graph: *warrant to a degree* δ and *ideal warrant* (Pollock 1995, p. 132f.). When G_0, G_1, G_2, ... is the sequence of partial inference graphs that are computed during reasoning, a conclusion is warranted to a degree δ if from *G*δ and up, the node corresponding to the conclusion is evaluated as justified. A conclusion is ideally warranted if the node corresponding to the conclusion is evaluated as justified in the union of all G_i. Pollock shows that the two notions do not coincide.

6.3.4 **Theory construction**

Pollock wants to build a system that can actually reason. As a result, he does not stop after providing a theory of the structure of defeasible reasoning (chapter 3 of Pollock 1995), and continues with the discussion of epistemic cognition (chapter 4).[6]

Pollock provides a model of how an artificial reasoner can try to settle issues given his beliefs. A straightforward approach would be to determine all the consequences from one's beliefs (cf., Pollock's theory of defeasible reasoning) and then check how the issues are answered. In practice an approach along such lines is not feasible, however. In general, the search space is enormous, often infinite.

[6] Pollock also describes how an agent can try to find courses of action to achieve his goals (in chapter 5 on plan-based practical reasoning), but that extends beyond the scope of the present book.

In order to manage the problem of computational complexity, Pollock proposes a bi-directional reasoning mechanism for settling issues from given beliefs. The idea is roughly that issues can be settled given certain beliefs by simultaneously reasoning forward from the given beliefs and backward from the issues. In his operationalization of this idea, Pollock assumes that rules of inference tend to be classifiable in those for forward reasoning and those for backward reasoning (Pollock 1995, p. 155). For instance, according to Pollock, *Modus ponens* (from φ and $\varphi \rightarrow \psi$, infer ψ) should provide forward reasons, whereas $\wedge$-*Introduction* (from φ and ψ, infer $\varphi \wedge \psi$)[7] should provide backward reasons.[8]

It is praiseworthy that Pollock attempts to manage the computational complexity of logical proof in his system. However, his proposal to classify rules of inference in forward and backward rules cannot work since it is easy to show that when the use of some rule of inference is limited to only forward or only backward reasoning, it can occur that fewer derivations can be made than without the limitation. In other words, an unwanted side-effect of Pollock's classification is that not all derivations can be constructed.

This can already be seen in a simple example. Assume that p, q and $p \wedge q \rightarrow r$ are given and that r is an issue to be settled. Clearly r follows from p, q and $p \wedge q \rightarrow r$ by one application of $\wedge$-*Introduction* followed by an application of *Modus ponens*. When *Modus ponens* only provides forward reasons and $\wedge$-*Introduction* only backward reasons (in accordance with the classification of these rules that Pollock finds plausible) it becomes impossible to show that the conclusion r follows from the assumptions on the basis of these two rules: a computation of a proof of r using p, q and $p \wedge q \rightarrow r$ in terms of *Modus ponens* and $\wedge$-*Introduction* will have to start by either applying *Modus ponens* backwardly or by applying $\wedge$-*Introduction* forwardly. As a result, the two-step derivation of r from p, q and $p \wedge q \rightarrow r$ cannot be constructed without violating Pollock's classification of rules of inference.

In general, all rules of inference can occur as the first rule in a derivation and as the last rule. When a rule of inference is the first one in a derivation, the computation of that derivation requires that the rule can be applied forwardly; and when a rule of inference is the last one in a derivation, it should

[7] The rule $\wedge$-*Introduction* is called 'adjunction' in Pollock's work.

[8] But note that Pollock formulates rules of inference in terms of sequents.

be possible to apply it backwardly. By restricting the use of rules of inference, Pollock has not only weeded out detours in derivations like p, $p \wedge p$, $p \wedge p \wedge p$, ... that are normally redundant, but also perfectly ordinary derivations.

In Pollock's architecture, the reasoning process can be controlled using the inference queue. At any stage of the reasoning process, the inference queue contains the inferences that can be made. The order of the elements of the queue depends on predefined preferences, e.g., in terms of the complexity of the sentences involved: reasoning with simpler sentences precedes reasoning with more complex sentences.

The reasoning mechanism of Pollock's OSCAR architecture is not meant to provide a model of theory construction. Pollock has focused on reasoning with the goal being to determine whether a fixed set of assumptions can (defeasibly) settle a fixed set of issues. In contrast, in theory construction assumptions and issues can be added and removed, and assumptions can be changed into issues or vice versa. Theory construction is not only a matter of settling given issues on the basis of given assumptions, but also a matter of finding the right assumptions and issues.

It would for instance be characteristic for theory construction when backward reasons could be used to provide a reason for a statement that was initially assumed (thereby turning the assumption into an issue). In Pollock's system, backward reasons are only used to replace an issue by a reason for it that might be easier to establish given the assumptions.

6.4 Vreeswijk's Abstract Argumentation Systems

In Vreeswijk's (1993, 1997) work on defeasible argumentation, the defeat of arguments is determined by the conflicts in which they are involved and by their conclusive force. Vreeswijk abstracts from the underlying language and conclusive force relation, by taking them as givens of a particular abstract argumentation system.

6.4.1 Arguing with pros and cons

In Vreeswijk's work, arguments are constructed from a given set of rules of inference, that are either strict or defeasible. Arguments are constructed by subordination, but not by coordination: the sentences in an argument cannot be supported by the application of several rules of inference at once.

When an argument is constructed using a defeasible rule of inference, the argument is defeasible. Vreeswijk uses an abstract, almost unstructured language with one distinguished sentence ⊥, expressing a contradiction. Contradiction indicates which arguments are incompatible: a set of arguments is incompatible when their conclusions lead to a contradiction. When arguments are incompatible with other arguments, they can become defeated. In Vreeswijk's argumentation theory, there is no direct representation of pros and cons, in the sense of reasons for and against a conclusion. Arguments are not dialectical, in the sense that they cannot contain both supporting and attacking reasons.

6.4.2 Arguing with warrants

Since Vreeswijk uses an abstract unstructured language, warrants are not explicitly modelled. Rules of inference are considered to be given. As a result, they can only be used to construct arguments, and cannot be derived.

In an appendix, Vreeswijk (1997, p. 274f.) discusses Pollock's rebutting and undercutting defeaters in terms of conditionals.

6.4.3 Argument evaluation

The mechanism of defeat that is used by Vreeswijk differs from the mechanism used in the systems proposed in this book. ARGUE! and ARGUMED all have a notion of counterargument that determines defeat: the idea is that an argument is defeated when there is a successful counterargument.

In Vreeswijk's abstract argumentation systems, the defeat of an argument is not the direct result of a counterargument, but of inconsistency in combination with conclusive force.[9] The starting point of Vreeswijk's ar-

[9] In other words, Vreeswijk's argumentation theory uses inconsistency-triggered defeat instead of counterargument-triggered defeat. Cf., the distinction between two types of defeat (Verheij 1996a, p. 164-165).

gumentation theory is that when there are defeasible arguments with conflicting conclusions, one of the arguments must be defeated.[10] So, when there are two defeasible arguments with opposing conclusions (and nothing is known about their conclusive force), there are two possibilities: either the first argument is defeated while the other is not, or vice versa. So, in general, a conflict of defeasible arguments leads to an ambiguous situation, with a number of possible options.

The number of options is constrained when there is information about the conclusive force of the arguments in a conflict. The idea is that when an argument that is involved in a conflict has stronger conclusive force than another argument in the conflict, the stronger argument is not the defeated one. So, in the case of two conflicting defeasible arguments one of which is stronger than the other, the ambiguity is resolved: the weaker argument is defeated and the stronger one is not.

Vreeswijk's theory assumes a two-layered view of defeasible reasoning (cf., also Prakken 1997 on argumentation layers). The first layer deals with the construction of arguments, the second with defeat. As a result, arguments themselves only represent the support relations between statements. There are no attack relations between statements.

6.4.4 Theory construction

Vreeswijk does not discuss theory construction in the sense of the process of finding the right premises and settling issues. Vreeswijk's theory assumes a fixed set of premises and all arguments are based in that set. There is no notion of issues. There is a discussion of the construction of extensions in terms of argumentation sequences. Such sequences consist of elementary argumentation steps. In such a step, at most one argument can be added and many deleted. According to Vreeswijk, argumentation sequences can under certain circumstances lead to the construction of extensions.

---

[10] Vreeswijk uses a somewhat different terminology. A key definition of Vreeswijk's theory is that of the extensions of a base set with respect to an argumentation system (1997, p. 249). In general, an extension need not contain all arguments based on the base set. It is natural to refer to those arguments as the defeated ones. Note that different extensions give rise to different sets of defeated arguments.

6.5 Prakken and Sartor's Winning strategies

Prakken and Sartor (1996) have provided a formal framework for the assessment of conflicting arguments. It is inspired by reasoning in the domain of law.

6.5.1 **Arguing with pros and cons**

Arguments are modelled as sequences of rules. Rules come in two forms: defeasible ones and strict ones. Formally, rules resemble those occurring in logic programming. However, rules have names in order to be able to refer to them. A typical example is the following (Prakken and Sartor 1996, p. 340):

r_1: ~x is a minor $\Rightarrow$ x has legal capacity

The rule, named r_1, expresses that someone has legal capacity unless he can be shown to be a minor. The negation is so-called weak negation: for the antecedent of the rule to be fulfilled it suffices that *there is no evidence* that x is a minor. The weakly negated sentence differs from its strongly negated counterpart (denoted $\neg x$ is a minor), which expresses that *it is not the case* that x is a minor.

Weak negation gives rise to one of the ways in which arguments can be defeated in Prakken and Sartor's theory, as follows. When a rule with an antecedent containing a weakly negated sentence is applied, that depends on an assumption of lacking evidence. Providing evidence to the contrary, e.g., in the example that x is a minor, counters that assumption. In other words, an argument for some conclusion is an argument against all arguments that are based on the application of a rule containing the weak negation of that conclusion. In this type of defeat, one of the assumptions of an argument is attacked.

The second way of defeat occurs when two arguments have opposite conclusions. In such a situation, rule priorities are used to compare the arguments in the conflict. In their 'Formal System II' (p. 352f.), Prakken and Sartor discuss reasoning concerning rule priorities. The names of rules are used for the expression of rule priority statements.

In Prakken and Sartor's (1996) theory, arguments (in the sense of derivations) can only be defeated as a whole. Attack cannot lead to the defeat of individual statements.

6.5.2 Arguing with warrants

The rules of Prakken and Sartor's (1996) theory can contain variables and can as such be thought of as warrants in the sense of generic support licences. There is no obvious distinction between support and attack licensing warrants, and there are no precluding warrants. Attack relations cannot be expressed as sentences and are therefore not a possible topic of argumentation. Attack between arguments depends on the input information, in the sense that the contingent priority information determines the attack relations actually available.

In an important way, Prakken and Sartor's rules are not like the warrants of Toulmin: it is not obvious how to express backings for them. The problem is that the rules are fixed in the input information and cannot be nested. As a result, it is not possible to provide reasons for a rule, which is the natural way to think of backings. Reasons against a warrant – not discussed by Toulmin – are similarly not immediately available in Prakken and Sartor's theory.

Prakken and Sartor discuss various ways of extending the basic language of their theory in order to express arguments that are characteristic for legal reasoning, such as reasoning concerning the applicability of a rule.

6.5.3 Argument evaluation

In Prakken and Sartor's (1996) theory, argument evaluation is determined in terms of winning strategies in dialogue games. The idea is that a statement is justified when a proponent of the statement can successfully defend it against the arguments of an opponent.

Prakken and Sartor deal with the construction of arguments and argument defeat in different layers. As a result, arguments contain support relations, but no attack relations.

6.5.4 Theory construction

Prakken and Sartor's (1996) theory does not treat theory construction. Although the theory is dialogue-based, it does not intend to model actual dialogues in which issues are settled by looking for the right premises. The dialogues are only used to define which statements are justified given the input information. Prakken and Sartor consider their theory to be a 'declarative', 'relational' approach to modeling legal argument, complementing a 'procedural' approach (cf., Prakken and Sartor 1996).

6.6 DUNG'S ADMISSIBLE SETS OF ARGUMENTS

Dung's (1993, 1995)[11] work provided an important abstraction of previous work, by focusing on the attack relation between arguments without considering argument structure at all. This has resulted in a significant clarification of many concepts related to defeasible reasoning. Dung focuses on different kinds of semantics for his argumentation frameworks and on relations with previous work on nonmonotonic reasoning and logic programming.

6.6.1 Arguing with pros and cons

The core of Dung's (1993, 1995) theory is an attack relation between arguments. As such, the theory focuses on attack and does not deal with support. Arguments are treated as unstructured givens. Since arguments are unstructured, they can in principle be placeholders for arguments-as-derivations and for arguments-as-statements. However, the applications that Dung gives of his theory suggest that he thinks of the arguments in his theory in the sense of derivations.

6.6.2 Arguing with warrants

Dung's arguments have no structure and do not consist of sentences of a

[11] Bondarenko, Dung, Kowalski and Toni (1997) have provided a theory that is formally closely related to Dung's (1993, 1995), but in which arguments have more structure. Kowalski and Toni (1996) provide applications to legal reasoning.

structured language. Since the expression of warrants requires a structured language, Dung's theory does not consider arguing with warrants.

6.6.3 **Argument evaluation**

An important part of Dung's (1993, 1995) work is his discussion of different kinds of semantics and the relations between them. For instance, a set of arguments (that does not contain arguments that attack each other) is called a stable extension when all arguments that are not in the set are attacked by an argument in the set. It is then natural to consider the arguments in the set as undefeated and the arguments outside the set as defeated with respect to the extension.[12] When a stable extension exists, all arguments can be evaluated as undefeated or defeated. However, it can occur that no stable extension exists or that there are several stable extensions.

When an argumentation framework has no stable extension, it can be the case that parts of the argumentation framework can be sensibly interpreted. Dung proposes the definition of admissible sets of arguments for that purpose. The definition of admissible sets makes the idea precise that the attack of an argument can become harmless when there is a counterattack, i.e., when the attacking argument is itself attacked. More precisely, a set of arguments (that does not contain arguments that attack each other) is admissible when all arguments that attack an argument in the set are themselves attacked by an argument in the set. An admissible set that contains as many arguments as possible – a so-called preferred extension – can be regarded as an interpretation of the argumentation framework in which as many arguments as possible are interpreted. The arguments in the preferred extension can be considered as undefeated with respect to the preferred extension, those attacked by the arguments in the set as defeated, while the remaining arguments remain unevaluated.

6.6.4 **Theory construction**

Dung's theory focuses on kinds of semantics and does not deal with procedural aspects of argumentation nor with theory construction.

---

[12] Dung (1993, 1995) does not define defeat status assignments. Verheij (1996b) connects Dung's set approach with a status assignment approach. See also Verheij (2000a).

6.7 CUMULA's Generalized Defeaters

CUMULA (Verheij 1996a, chapters 5 and 6) is a formal model of argumentation with defeasible arguments. Argumentation is considered to take place in stages. In subsequent stages, new arguments are taken into account, and this influences the status of the arguments: an argument that is justified in a stage can become defeated in a subsequent stage, and vice versa. CUMULA focuses on the relation between the reason structure of arguments and defeat. It is discussed here since the argumentation theory underlying the ARGUE! System was inspired by CUMULA.

6.7.1 Arguing with pros and cons

In CUMULA (Verheij 1996a), arguments are tree-like structures of reasons and conclusions. As a result, CUMULA's arguments are arguments in the sense of derivations. Arguments can however not only be constructed by the subordination of argument steps, but also by coordination. In other words: argument steps can be combined in parallel. As a result, a conclusion can be supported by several independent reasons. In logic, derivations can normally not be constructed by coordination. Coordination is used in the well-established argumentation theory by Van Eemeren et al. (1981, 1987).[13]

In CUMULA, all reasons in an argument are supporting reasons. Arguments can be attacked by other arguments. Attack is represented by defeaters. A defeater consists of a set of attacking arguments and a set of attacked arguments.

6.7.2 Arguing with warrants

CUMULA does not specify the language in which the statements that form arguments are expressed. As a result, CUMULA does not model warrants.

[13] However, there is a difference in terminology: when independent reasons are combined in parallel, Van Eemeren et al. (1981, 1987) speak of multiple arguments. When a number of subreasons in combination form one reason, they speak of coordinated arguments.

6.7.3 Argument evaluation

CumulA's attack (modelled in terms of defeaters) can lead to the defeat of arguments: when the attacking arguments of a defeater are undefeated, the attacked arguments are defeated. In terms of defeaters, several kinds of defeat can be distinguished. For instance, next to undercutting and rebutting defeat – in a sense derived from Pollock's (1987) – it is possible to distinguish defeat by sequential weakening and defeat by parallel strengthening.

The evaluation of arguments is defined in terms of argumentation stages. Each stage represents which arguments are taken into account and what their evaluation status is. Arguments are either undefeated or defeated at each stage. It may be thought that it suffices to represent a stage of argumentation in terms of only the arguments that are undefeated at the stage. This comes down to 'forgetting' the arguments that are defeated. This is unwanted since during a line of argumentation arguments can change status repeatedly. When defeated arguments are forgotten, they must again be taken into account in order to reinstate them.

6.7.4 Theory construction

In CumulA, argumentation is considered as a process that takes place in stages. Argumentation stages are chained in lines of argumentation, as a representation of the process of argumentation. Premises can change during a line of argumentation. Issues are not distinguished.

6.8 Reason-Based Logic

Reason-Based Logic, as initiated by Hage, and further developed in cooperation with Verheij (Hage 1996, 1997; Verheij 1996a), can be characterized as a theory of rules and reasons. It does not have an explicit notion of an argument.[14] Instead it focuses on types of sentences related to rules and reasons, and on the states of affairs expressed by sentences of these types.

[14] As such Reason-Based Logic is the odd one out in the list of theories of defeasible argumentation discussed in this chapter.

Reason-Based Logic is of special relevance here, since the argumentation theories underlying ARGUMED 2.0 and ARGUMED 3.0, have resulted from attempts to bridge the unsatisfactory conceptual gap between Reason-Based Logic and CUMULA, as occurred in my dissertation (Verheij 1996a). The discussion below is based on the version of Reason-Based Logic presented by Verheij (1996a).

6.8.1 Arguing with pros and cons

In Reason-Based Logic, it is possible to express which facts are reasons for or against other facts. Reasons are the result of the application of rules. Rules normally apply when their conditions are satisfied, but the application of a rule can be excluded in case of an exclusionary reason. It can occur that there are conflicting reasons. In that case, a conclusion can only be drawn after considering the relative weight of the pros and cons.

6.8.2 Arguing with warrants

Reason-Based Logic's rules (or perhaps its rule validities) are comparable to warrants. By the richness of the language of Reason-Based Logic, it is possible to express different kinds of warrant-like statements. For instance, it is possible to express that some fact can provide a reason against a rule's validity.

6.8.3 Argument evaluation

The definition of extensions in Reason-Based Logic (in the style of Reiter 1980) can be regarded as a definition of the statements justified with respect to a given set of assumptions. Assumptions are not prima facie and issues are not distinguished.

6.8.4 Theory construction

Reason-Based Logic (Verheij 1996a) only defines which consequences can be drawn from a given theory. How to arrive at a theory is not discussed. There is related work on Reason-Based Logic that deals with the setting of dialogues (Hage, Leenes, Lodder 1994; Lodder 1998). In that work, the dialogue participants can become committed to the statements which they make. In this way, the so-called commitment stores of the participants change during a dialogue. Such evolving commitment stores are conceptually related to gradually constructed theories.

6.9 ARGUE!, ARGUMED 2.0 AND ARGUMED 3.0

In the following, an overview is given of the main findings of the argumentation theories of ARGUE!, ARGUMED 2.0 and ARGUMED 3.0 with respect to our four points of focus.

6.9.1 **Arguing with pros and cons**

- A major difference between the argumentation theories underlying the systems is that in ARGUE! defeat is a property of arguments (in the sense of reason-conclusion structures) whereas in the ARGUMED systems defeat is a property of statements. Likewise, in ARGUE! attack is a relation between arguments, while in the ARGUMED systems attack is a relation between statements.

  A statement-oriented approach seems to be more natural than a derivation-oriented approach. In argument assistants, a statement-oriented approach provides a representation of arguing with pros and cons that is more easily recognizable by users. Examples of statement-based approaches to attack and defeat are Toulmin's argument scheme, Reiter's logic for default reasoning and DEFLOG. Examples of derivation-oriented approaches are Pollock's rebutting and undercutting defeaters,[15] Vreeswijk's abstract argumentation systems, Prakken and Sartor's winning strategies and CUMULA. Dung's admissible sets of arguments can be interpreted as a statement-oriented and as a derivation-oriented approach, although Dung's work suggests that he thinks of his theory in terms of derivations.[16] Reason-Based Logic does not explicitly provide an approach to attack and defeat.

---

[15] Note that Pollock defines defeat status assignments on inference graphs that are constructed from sequents. Cf., section 6.3.

[16] In an appendix (section B.3), it is shown that Dung's approach can be interpreted in terms of statements by embedding it in DEFLOG.

- A statement-oriented approach to dialectical argumentation allows the distinction between different kinds of attack, such as undercutters and rebutters. This becomes possible when conditional relations between statements can be expressed (cf., what is said below on arguing with warrants).

6.9.2 Arguing with warrants

- ArguMed 3.0 based on DefLog shows that Toulmin's warrants can be analyzed in terms of nested support. A warrant is then regarded as a reason for the supporting connection between a reason and the conclusion it supports. Similarly, Pollock's undercutters can be analyzed in terms of nested attack. An undercutter is then a reason against the supporting connection between a reason and the conclusion it supports. In this sense, Toulmin's warrants are support licences, and Pollock's undercutters support preclusions.
- There are two straightforward generalizations of Toulmin's warrants and Pollock's undercutters: attack licences and attack preclusions. The former are reasons for the attacking connection between a reason and the conclusion which it attacks, the latter are reasons against such attacking connections. These generalizations occur in actual argumentation. For instance, in the law the issue of whether or not some statement is a reason against another statement can be the subject of debate. There can of course be both reasons for and reasons against that issue. Using the formal notation of the logical system DefLog (that underlies ArguMed 3.0), the following provides an overview of the four possibilities:

$w \leadsto (p \leadsto q)$	support licence (warrant): w licenses that p supports q
$w \leadsto (p \leadsto \times q)$	attack licence: w licenses that p attacks q
$u \leadsto \times(p \leadsto q)$	support preclusion (undercutter): u precludes that p supports q
$u \leadsto \times(p \leadsto \times q)$	attack preclusion: u precludes that p attacks q

6.9.3 Argument evaluation

- The argument assistants Argue!, ArguMed 2.0 and ArguMed 3.0 all allow the evaluation of argumentative data. This is essential for data concerning defeasible arguments and statements. Several other systems stop at the graphical representation of the data (e.g., Belvedere by Suthers et al. 1995, and systems based on Toulmin 1958, who did not discuss argument evaluation; see Verheij 2001a). A difficulty is of course that there is no consensus with respect to defeasible argumentation and its (formal) evaluation. DefLog has been designed in order to be as transparent as possible with respect to the evaluation of dialectical arguments based on prima facie justified assumptions.

6.9.4 Theory construction

- ArguMed 3.0 can be regarded as a dialectical theory construction tool. Issues can be raised and assumptions can be made in order to settle the issues. However, assumptions are considered to be only prima facie justified. When an assumption is successfully attacked by a reason against it, it becomes defeated. It is also possible to change assumptions to issues and vice versa. As a result, by the critical scrutiny of the assumptions and providing reasons for and against them, a theory settling the issues can be constructed gradually.
- The main characteristics of theory construction as used in ArguMed 3.0 are its use of a logical language that can express support and attack between statements in terms of conditionals and its distinction between assumptions and issues. It is accompanied by a transparent definition of argument evaluation, the core of which can be summarized as follows: a statement is justified if it is supported by the justified assumptions, and a statement is defeated if it is attacked by them.

Chapter 7
Argument Assistants: Conclusions and Prospects

Chapter 7
Argument Assistants: Conclusions and Prospects

The argument assistants described in this book are obviously experimental. In their present form, it is not to be expected that they will be widely used for engaging in argumentation. There are good reasons why it is the case that the development of argument assistants for defeasible argumentation is still in an experimental phase. A first difficulty is the lack of a canonical theory of defeasible argumentation, and more specifically of legal argumentation.[1] A second difficulty is that argument assistants require the design of user interfaces of a new kind. There is still much to be learnt about the way arguments can be sensibly and clearly presented to the users (especially when they are defeasible), or with the way argument moves should be performed by the user. Difficulties such as these could be the cause of the striking differences between the argumentation theories and user interfaces of argument assistants (see chapter 5 on argument assistants and chapter 6 on theories of defeasible argumentation).

Elsewhere (Verheij 1998a, 1998b), I have argued that even in the current experimental phase the development of argument assistance systems is relevant. I distinguished four ways in which the development of argument assistance systems is worthwhile: first, such systems can serve as *realizations* of (formal) argumentation theories, which is especially relevant because of the (well-recognized) technical difficulties of many theories; second, they are *testbeds* for argumentation theories, technically, philosophically and in practice; third, argument assistants can be *showcases*, giving the argumentation theories more credibility; and, finally, they can be *practical aids*, with applications in, e.g., legal decision-making, planning and education. Currently developed systems are already worthwhile in the first two, more theoretically oriented ways, and are starting to become so in the second two, more practically oriented ways.

[1] For an overview of argument models in the law, see, e.g., Bench-Capon (1997) and the special issue of *Artificial Intelligence and Law*, Vol. 4, Nos. 3/4, 1996. For overviews of defeasible argumentation, see, e.g., Prakken and Vreeswijk (2002), or Chesñevar, Maguitman and Loui (2000). For an overview of nonmonotonic logics, see Gabbay, Hogger and Robinson (1994).

In the following, the results and conclusions of the development of ARGUE! and the ARGUMED family are summarized. First, a brief overview is given of the systems themselves (section 7.1). Section 7.2 deals with the prospects of argument assistants.

7.1 OVERVIEW OF ARGUE!, ARGUMED 2.0 AND ARGUMED 3.0

With respect to the three argument assistants discussed in this book, the following can be concluded.

ARGUE!, the system that was developed first, provides an interesting realization of (and a testbed for) a particular theory of defeasible argumentation (a stripped-down version of CUMULA; Verheij 1996a), but that theory is not sufficiently natural to apply to ordinary argumentation. Its user interface, which allows the user to draw and organize argumentative data on screen, is flexible, but is also made cumbersome by the complexity of the data structures (especially of the defeaters). As such, it is mainly relevant from a research perspective. For instance, its step by step evaluation function provides interesting insights into the evaluation of defeasible arguments.

ARGUMED 2.0 is much more easily accessible for ordinary users. This has been qualitatively corroborated by a user evaluation (section 1.5). Its model and representation of undercutting exceptions and the resulting effects on statement evaluation turned out to be natural and easy to understand. The addition of step and undercutter warrants made the argumentation theory significantly richer, but their representation and the way they had to be handled in the system turned out to be obstacles for several users. The use of the template-based interface was easily learnt by autonomous exploration, but had the drawback that it was difficult to connect the argumentative data filled in on the template form with what was happening in the argument screen.

ARGUMED 3.0 simplified the warrant model of ARGUMED 2.0 by considering the arrows between a reason and its (supported or attacked) conclusion as conditional statements. The result was an expressive and flexible argumentation theory (formalized as the logical system DEFLOG). The evaluation function became logically more satisfactory (with respect to that of ARGUMED 2.0) by its correspondence to DEFLOG. As a user interface, a middle way was taken between the too flexible interface of ARGUE! and the too rigid one of ARGUMED 2.0. This has been achieved by the use of a mouse-sensitive argument screen in which the argumentative data is organized by the system. Editing the argumentative data occurs directly on the argument screen, instead of in separate template forms.

Sections 5.7 and 6.9 summarize how the systems' design and argumentation theories relate to other work.

7.2 CONTRIBUTIONS AND CONCLUSIONS

The main contributions of the research presented in this book are the following:

- Three argument assistants that model defeasible argumentation in the law have been presented: ARGUE!, ARGUMED 2.0 and ARGUMED 3.0.
- Graphical representations of defeasible argumentation have been introduced, both for an argument-based approach to defeasible argumentation (in ARGUE!) and for a statement-based approach (in the ARGUMED systems).
- Two kinds of interface for argument assistants have been implemented: a structure-centred interface in which graphical structures are drawn (in ARGUE!) and a move-centred interface in which users make argumentation moves. The move-centred interface came in two styles: one used template forms (ARGUMED 2.0), the other a mouse-sensitive screen (ARGUMED 3.0).
- A statement-based theory of defeasible argumentation has been presented. It was implemented in ARGUMED 3.0 and formalized as DEFLOG. This is in contrast to the more common argument-based theories. DEFLOG provides a theory of prima facie justified assumptions. Formally, DEFLOG is related to Dung's work on argumentation systems.
- A unified, conditional-based interpretation of Toulmin's warrants and Pollock's undercutters has been presented (in terms of DEFLOG).
- Two kinds of argument evaluation have been implemented: a step by step evaluation (ARGUE!) and global evaluation (ARGUMED). In ARGUMED 3.0, the system computes all possible evaluations, sometimes none, sometimes several (cf., the non-existence and multiplicity of extensions in nonmonotonic logics).

The following can be concluded:

- Theories of defeasible argumentation in the law can be the basis of usable and comprehensible argument assistants.
- Argument assistants can be used for free argumentation (instead of premise-based or issue-based approaches) about the application of law to cases. As such, they are theory construction tools.
- The user interface of an argument assistant should be move-centred and not structure-centred. When moves are entered using template forms, users easily become lost. Direct interaction with the graphically represented arguments using a mouse-sensitive screen is better in this respect.
- User evaluation showed that some test persons understood and used all types of moves and evaluation in ArguMed 2.0 and ArguMed 3.0 as intended without much training. Autonomous exploration and the presentation of a single example of each type sufficed. All test persons understood and used the simplest argument moves, namely making statements, and giving a supporting or attacking reason. Undercutting was somewhat more difficult, but was still understood and used by most test persons. The distinction between issues and assumptions, especially in relation to argument evaluation, was reported as the most difficult element of the argumentation theory. Also warranting turned out to be relatively difficult. Interestingly, most test persons understood the examples of warranting and could reproduce them, but subsequently did not use warranting when asked to represent a given textual argument in the graphical format of the argument assistants.
- Statement-based theories of defeasible argumentation are more natural than argument-based theories.
- Toulmin's warrants and Pollock's undercutters can be modelled in a unified way in terms of a statement-based theory of defeasible argumentation.

7.3 Future Research and Prospects

Many questions remain open or have not or have hardly been addressed. Let us discuss some of them, as an indication of research questions to be addressed in the future.

- What kind of argumentation support is useful for which arguers under what circumstances? It seems obvious that different kinds of arguers have different needs under different circumstances. For instance, a novice arguer in some field (like a first-year law student) will need another type of support than an expert arguer.
- How can aspects of argumentation other than those discussed in this book be usefully modelled by argument assistants? One can for instance think of dialogue aspects of argumentation, including discussion rules, fallacy detection and reasoning on the basis of argumentation schemes.
- Is it useful to develop argument assistants that are adapted to specific contexts of argumentation? One can think of systems for courtroom debate, deliberation by decision-makers and skills training tools. For instance, it might be useful to provide support for domain-specific argumentation schemes, such as the typically legal kinds of argumentation involving precedents, rules, principles, values and goals.
- In what kind of format must argumentation be presented? There is the main dichotomy between graphical representations and textual representations, but also in those two groups many variants are conceivable. The complexities and subtleties of argument, for instance in the law, may impede graphical representations, and require natural language representations. A compromise could be the dual representation of arguments, both graphically and in natural language.
- Should the argumentation theory underlying an argument assistant correspond to actual human argumentation? In other words, should an argument assistant correspond to empirically validated models of argumentation? Or do idealizations of actual argumentation lead to more useful assistance? If the correspondence is too close, the model would include typical errors made by humans, but if the correspondence is too weak, users cannot connect the model with their own argumentative practices.
- Is the automatic or semi-automatic evaluation of argumentation an effective tool? What kind of information concerning argument evaluation is relevant for a user?
- Is the labelling of statement and move types useful? For instance, systems using Toulmin's scheme have the advantage that the different slots in the scheme are assigned specific argumentative roles, such as warrant and backing. This can have the effect that a user is forced to better orga-

nize his argumentation. However, a drawback is that the assigned roles may lead to argumentative rigidity.

- How can domain knowledge be usefully integrated in argument assistants? The inclusion of more content in argument assistants can become the most important direction of future research. This will lead to diminishing the gap between argument assistants and automated reasoners. Argument assistants have the advantage of being open and flexible, but it is to be expected that the integration of domain knowledge can make the systems more useful in practice. In this way, the advantages of both argument assistants and automated reasoners become available.

The present state of research is only a first step towards answering questions like the above. It is a challenge to continue the development of argument assistants and to turn them into valuable knowledge management tools of a new kind. It is exciting to imagine how argument assistants can change the argumentation practice in argument-intensive environments, such as the law.

Let us finish with two succinct and thought-provoking statements by test persons. One test person – a full professor of civil law – posited that he had the impression that only about 10% of what counts in legal argumentation could be captured in formally-oriented systems like ARGUMED. Another test person – a young attorney at law – said that the ARGUMED system had changed his view of the law. Both statements can provide inspiration for further research.

Appendix A
The test protocol of ARGUMED 2.0 (translated excerpt)

C.1 Start the ARGUMED program by double-clicking the ARGUMED icon.

You will see the following:

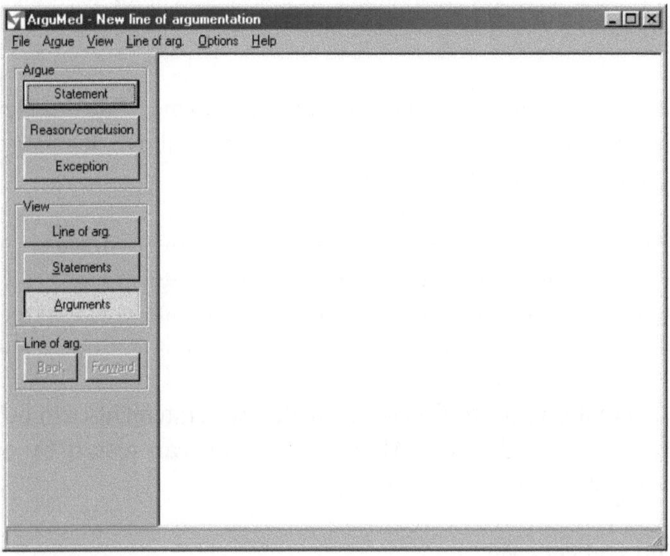

C.2 Open the file 'line_of_argumentation01.lin' by choosing 'File' – 'Open...' in the menu. The following will appear:

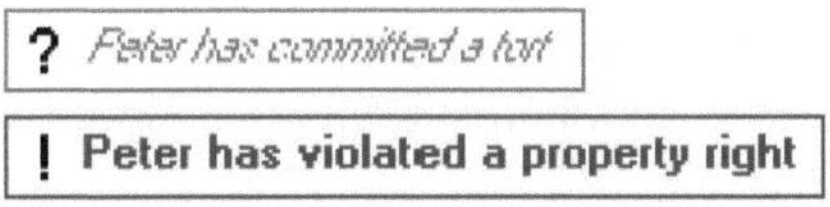

Two statements are graphically represented. They are represented differently. For instance, you can see a question mark and an exclamation mark.

C.3 Do you have any idea what can be meant by the differences? If so, what is your hypothesis?
(Note: For this research your first impressions are relevant, much more so than the intended answer to a question. Therefore your answers can never be 'wrong'.)

....
....
....
....

C.4 Start a new line of argumentation by clicking 'File' – 'New' in the menu. Try to reproduce the two statements above, keeping their different representations in mind.

....
....
....
....

The idea is that you try to find out how the two statements can be made by experimenting with the ArguMed system. You can restart by opening a new file (by clicking 'File' – 'New').

C.5 Did you succeed?

□ Yes.
□ No. Please explain why.

....
....
....
....

You can enter statements by clicking the 'Statement' button in the area labelled 'Argue'. The following form will appear:

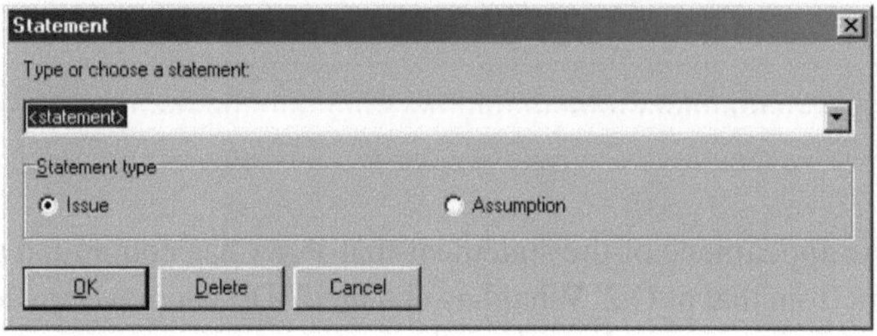

You can make a statement by typing a sentence on the completion line and then clicking the OK button.

In the argumentation theory underlying ARGUMED, statements have a ***type***. A statement can be an *issue* or an *assumption*. On the statement form you can indicate the type of your statement.

An exclamation mark indicates a statement of the assumption type, a question mark a statement of the issue type.

C.6 At C.3 you were asked to provide a hypothesis concerning the different representations of the two statements. Would you now give a different answer? If so, which?

C.7 Open the file 'line_of_argumentation02.lin'. You will see the following:

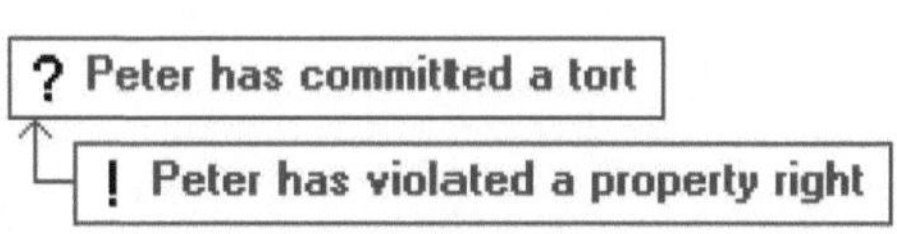

A simple argument is represented. Please state the argument in your own words.

....
....
....
....

C.8 The appearance of the statement that Peter has committed a tort differs from that at C.2. What has changed? Do you have any idea why? If so, what is your hypothesis?

....
....
....
....

C.9 Open the file 'line_of_argumentation01.lin'. Try to produce the argument of C.7.

C.10 Did you succeed?

□ Yes.
□ No. Try to indicate why.

....
....
....
....

Appendix B
Spin-off: the dialectical logic DEFLOG

DEFLOG is the formal version of the argumentation theory underlying the argument assistant ARGUMED 3.0 (see section 4.1.4). This appendix contains some further information concerning DEFLOG. The notion of dialectical justification is defined and is shown to lead to a criterion for the existence and multiplicity of dialectical interpretations. A formal connection is established between DEFLOG and Dung's (1995) argumentation frameworks. Further details on DEFLOG are provided by Verheij (2000a, 2003a).

B.1 DIALECTICALLY JUSTIFYING ARGUMENTS

Before we proceed to the notion of dialectical justification, some terminology needs to be introduced.

(i) A set of sentences is an *argument* when it is conflict-free. If Δ is a set of sentences, a *Δ-argument* is an argument that is a subset of Δ.
(ii) Let φ be a sentence. An argument C is an *argument for* φ if C supports φ. An argument C is an *argument against* φ if C attacks φ. The sentences in an argument C are also called its *premises*, the sentences φ such that C supports φ, its *conclusions*.
(iii) An argument C *attacks* an argument C' if C attacks a sentence in C'.
(iv) Arguments C and C' are *compatible* when $C \cup C'$ is an argument, and otherwise they are *incompatible*. The arguments in a collection $\{C_i\}_{i \in I}$ are *compatible* if their union $\cup_{i \in I} C_i$ is an argument, otherwise they are *incompatible*.

In the following figure, three arguments are graphically suggested.

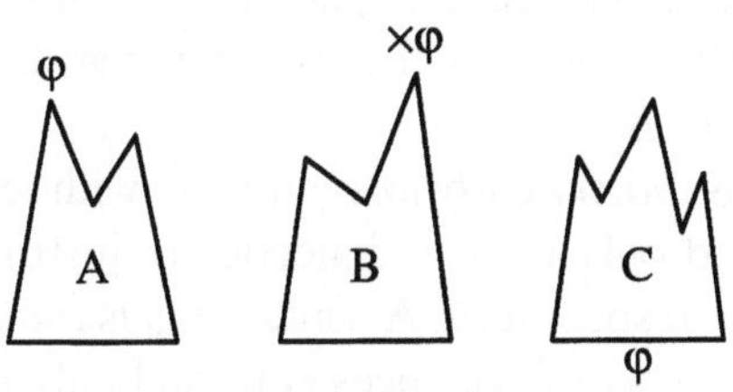

Figure B.1: Three arguments

The bases of the alpine shapes consist of the premises of the argument; the summits form the conclusions. Argument A has conclusion φ, argument B conclusion ×φ and argument C has premise φ. B attacks C, but not necessarily A (since φ might not be a premise of A). A and B are incompatible, as are B and C.

When a theory has a dialectical interpretation, the set of sentences of the theory that are justified in the interpretation are clearly an argument. It has a special property:

Proposition (1)

Let E be an extension of a theory Δ. Then J(E) ∩ Δ is a Δ-argument that attacks any Δ-argument C that is incompatible with J(E) ∩ Δ. Here J(E) denotes the set of justified statements of the extension E.

Proof: Since E is an extension, J(E) ∩ Δ is conflict-free. Hence a Δ-argument C that is incompatible with J(E) ∩ Δ cannot be a subset of J(E) ∩ Δ since J(E) ∩ Δ is not incompatible with any of its subsets. Therefore there is a sentence φ in C that is not in J(E) ∩ Δ. Since E is an extension, it is in D(E), the set of defeated sentences of the extension E. But for any sentence φ in D(E) it is evident due to the definition of extensions that J(E) ∩ Δ attacks φ, and therefore attacks C.

Arguments with the property that J(E) ∩ Δ has in proposition (1) above are said to be dialectically justifying:

(v) A Δ-argument C is *dialectically justifying* with respect to Δ if, and only if, C attacks any Δ-argument C' that is incompatible with C.

(vi) A sentence φ is *dialectically justifiable* with respect to a set of sentences Δ if, and only if, there is a Δ-argument C for φ that is dialectically justifying with respect to Δ. Such an argument C is then called a *dialectical justification of* φ, and C *dialectically justifies* φ with respect to Δ. A sentence φ is *dialectically defeasible* with respect to Δ if, and only if, ×φ is dialectically justifiable with respect to Δ. If C is a dialectical justification of φ, then the argument C *dialectically defeats* φ with respect to Δ.

(vii) A sentence φ is *dialectically interpretable* with respect to a set of sentences Δ if, and only if, it is dialectically justifiable or dialectically defeasible with respect to Δ. A sentence φ is *dialectically ambiguous* with respect to a set of sentences Δ if, and only if, it is both dialectically justifiable and dialectically defeasible with respect to Δ.

The argument $\{p, r, r \rightsquigarrow \times q\}$ dialectically justifies p with respect to the theory $\{p, q, r, q \rightsquigarrow \times p, r \rightsquigarrow \times q\}$. The argument $\{p\}$ does not dialectically justify p since the incompatible argument $\{q, q \rightsquigarrow \times p\}$ is not attacked. The argument $\{r, r \rightsquigarrow \times q\}$ dialectically defeats q with respect to the theory.

The sentences p and q are dialectically ambiguous with respect to the theory $\{p, q, p \rightsquigarrow \times q, q \rightsquigarrow \times p\}$ since the argument $\{p, p \rightsquigarrow \times q\}$ dialectically justifies p and dialectically defeats q, and likewise for q.

The sentence p is not dialectically interpretable with respect to the theory $\{p, p \rightsquigarrow \times p\}$.

Note that when an argument is dialectically justifying with respect to a theory, it dialectically justifies all the sentences it supports.

B.2 The Existence and Multiplicity of Extensions

When a theory has a dialectical interpretation, all sentences in the theory are dialectically interpretable. In other words, dialectical justification is a kind of 'local' dialectical interpretation. This is an immediate corollary of proposition (1) proven in section B.1:

Corollary (2)

Let E be an extension of the theory Δ. Then all sentences in the theory are dialectically justifiable or dialectically defeasible with respect to Δ.

Proof: By proposition (1) in section B.1, $J(E) \cap \Delta$ dialectically justifies or defeats all sentences in Δ.

Note that corollary (2) gives a necessary condition for the existence of an extension: when there is a sentence in a theory that is not dialectically interpretable, there cannot be an extension. Corollary (2) can explain all examples of theories without extensions that have been encountered above: in all, there is a sentence that is not dialectically interpretable. Nevertheless, the condition in corollary (2) is *not* sufficient for the existence of an extension, as the theory $\Delta = \{p, q, p \rightsquigarrow \times q, q \rightsquigarrow \times p, r, r \rightsquigarrow \times r, s, s \rightsquigarrow \times s, p \rightsquigarrow \times r, q \rightsquigarrow \times s\}$ shows. It has no extension. Nevertheless all sentences in the theory are dialectically justifiable or defeasible with respect to Δ. The Δ-argument $\{p, p \rightsquigarrow \times q, p \rightsquigarrow \times r\}$ dialectically justifies p and dialectically defeats q and r, while $\{q, q \rightsquigarrow \times p, q \rightsquigarrow \times s\}$ dialectically justifies q and dialectically defeats p and r.

The notion of dialectical justification plays a central role in the main theorem (3) below, that shows exactly under which circumstances a theory has an extension. One additional definition is needed.

(viii) Let C be an argument. A sentence φ is *dialectically justifiable in the context* C with respect to a theory Δ if it is supported by a dialectically justifying argument of the theory that contains C, and *dialectically defeasible in the context* C if ×φ is supported by a dialectically justifying argument that contains C.

Now the main theorem can be formulated:

Theorem (3)

A theory Δ has an extension if, and only if, there is an argument C in the context of which all sentences in Δ are either dialectically justifiable or dialectically defeasible with respect to the theory, but not both.

(The proof follows below.) In other words, a theory has an extension if, and only if, there is a context in which all sentences of the theory are dialectically interpretable, while none are dialectically ambiguous. Theorem (3) is closely related to corollary (2) above that says that the dialectical interpretability of all sentences of a theory is necessary for the existence of an extension. Theorem (3) says that the dialectical interpretability of all sentences *in a context with no dialectical ambiguities* is both necessary and sufficient for the existence of an extension. After fixing all choices allowed by a dialectically ambiguous sentence in the theory, it suffices for the existence of an extension that all sentences in the theory are either dialectically justifiable or dialectically defeasible. The example that showed why the dialectical interpretability of all sentences of a theory is not sufficient for the existence of an extension, shows what can go wrong: the dialectical justification of one sentence (or its dialectical negation) need not be compatible with that of another when there is dialectical ambiguity. In other words, the dialectical justification of sentences can depend on the particular choice allowed by a dialectical ambiguity. Dialectical justifications that require different choices cannot be 'glued' to form an extension.

Three properties of dialectical justification are essential in the proof of the theorem (3):

Proposition (4)

(i) *Localization:* Let E be an extension of a theory Δ. Then there is a collection $\{C_i\}_{i \in I}$ of arguments that cover J(E) ∩ Δ (i.e., J(E) ∩ Δ is equal to $\cup_{i \in I} C_i$), that are dialectically justifying with respect to the theory.

(ii) *Union:* If C and C' are compatible arguments, that are dialectically justifying with respect to a theory Δ, then also C ∪ C' is dialectically justifying with respect to the theory. (Similarly, for collections of dialectically justifying arguments: the union of a compatible collection of dialectically justifying arguments is again dialectically justifying.)

(iii) *Separation at the base:*[1] If C and C' are incompatible arguments, that are dialectically justifying with respect to a theory Δ, then there is a sentence in Δ that is both dialectically justifiable and defeasible with respect to Δ. (Similarly, for collections of dialectically justifying arguments: given an incompatible collection of dialectically justifying arguments, there is a sentence in the theory that is both dialectically justifiable and defeasible.)

Proof: Localization follows from proposition (1): it shows that J(E) ∩ Δ is itself dialectically justifying with respect to Δ. The union property (for pairs of arguments) is seen as follows. Let C and C' be compatible dialectically justifying arguments, and let the argument C" be incompatible with C ∪ C'. Assume, first, that C" is incompatible with C. Then clearly C attacks C". Assume, second, that C" is compatible with C. Then C' is incompatible with the argument C ∪ C", and therefore it attacks the argument. Since C and C' are compatible, it then follows that C' attacks C". The proof of the general case of the union property requires some extra care, but is similar. The property of separation at the base follows directly from the definition of dialectical justification: when C and C' are dialectically justifying and incompatible, they attack each other. Then there is a sentence in each (and therefore in the theory itself) that is attacked by the other. The general case of the separation property can be reduced to the case of pairs of arguments.
Proof of the main theorem (3): First let E be an extension of Δ. Then by the localization property J(E) ∩ Δ can be covered by arguments that are dialectically justifying with respect to Δ. By the union property, it then follows that J(E) ∩ Δ is also dialectically justifying. (In fact, the proof of corollary (2) directly shows that J(E) ∩ Δ is dialectically justifying.) As a result, J(E) ∩ Δ is a context as in theorem (3) since by the fact that J(E) ∩ Δ is dialectically justifying and by the definition of extensions all sentences in Δ are dialectically interpretable in the context of J(E) ∩ Δ, and since by the fact

[1] The property is called separation *at the base* since the dialectically ambiguous sentence can be found in the theory itself.

that J(E) $\cap$ Δ is conflict-free there is no dialectically ambiguous sentence in that context. Second let C be a context as in theorem (3), and let, for all sentences φ, C_φ be a Δ-argument dialectically justifying or defeating φ in the context C. The collection of C_φ are compatible since by the property of separation at the base there would otherwise be a sentence in the theory that is dialectically ambiguous in the context C. By the union property, the union of the C_φ is dialectically justifying. It specifies an extension of Δ.

The proof shows that extensions can be built by 'gluing' dialectically justifying arguments. This suggests that a (set-theoretically minimal) argument that dialectically justifies a sentence, is a kind of dialectical proof of the sentence. Similarly, such a dialectical proof of the dialectical negation of a sentence is a kind of dialectical refutation of the sentence.

The following theorem provides a general answer to the extension existence and multiplicity problems in the context of dialectical argumentation. It follows from the main theorem (3) above:

Theorem (5)

Let *n* be a natural (or cardinal) number (possibly 0). A theory Δ has exactly *n* extensions if, and only if, *n* is equal to the maximal number of mutually incompatible arguments C in the context of which all sentences in Δ are either dialectically justifiable or dialectically defeasible with respect to the theory, but not both.

B.3 Dung's Argumentation Frameworks and Admissibility

Dung's (1995) argumentation frameworks are a fruitful abstraction of ideas from nonmonotonic reasoning and logic programming. Here it is shown how Dung's argumentation frameworks can be mimicked in DefLog. In fact, it is shown that Dung's argumentation frameworks can be naturally regarded as DefLog theories that only use sentences of a subset of DefLog's language. Since Dung has shown that his argumentation frameworks have close formal connections with well-established models of defeasible reasoning, such as Reiter's (1980) default logic and logic programming, the results on DefLog presented here become of direct relevance for these models. Moreover, it is shown why Dung's notion of admissibility cannot in general replace that of dialectical justification in the characterizations of the existence and of the number of extensions of a theory proven above.

Formally, an argumentation framework consists of a set, its elements called *arguments*, and a binary relation on that set, the *attack* relation. When (A, B) is in the attack relation, the argument A is said to attack B.

In Dung's work, the notion of admissibility is central. It is closely related to DEFLOG's dialectical justification. Using DEFLOG's terminology, an argument C is *admissible* with respect to a theory Δ if C attacks any Δ-argument attacking it. This definition of admissibility depends of course on DEFLOG's particular notions of argument and attack. There is, however, a straightforward way of mimicking Dung's argumentation frameworks in DEFLOG for which this definition of admissibility is indeed an extrapolation of Dung's admissibility, as follows.

Let each argument of an argumentation framework be an elementary sentence in DEFLOG's language. Then an argumentation framework can be translated to a theory in DEFLOG by taking the union of the set of arguments in the framework and the set of sentences of the form $A \leadsto \times B$, for any element (A, B) of the attack relation of the framework. In addition, it is easy to restrict DEFLOG's language in such a way that any theory in this restricted language corresponds to an argumentation framework in Dung's sense: simply allow only elementary sentences and sentences of the form $\varphi \leadsto \times\psi$, where φ and ψ are elementary. Let us call sentences in this restricted sense *Dung sentences* and theories consisting of Dung sentences *Dung theories*.

It is now straightforward to check that several of Dung's notions coincide with DEFLOG's under this translation. Some care is needed, however, since certain terms have different meanings in Dung's work and in DEFLOG. For instance, the use of the term 'argument' is different. However, conflict-free sets of arguments (in Dung's sense) correspond with conflict-free sets of Dung sentences (in DEFLOG's sense), Dung's admissible sets of arguments correspond to the admissible arguments of Dung theories (in DEFLOG's sense), and Dung's stable extensions of argumentation frameworks correspond with DEFLOG's extensions of Dung theories. In an extended manuscript (Verheij 2000a), these results were formally established.

For theories using DEFLOG's full language, dialectical justification and admissibility are easily seen to be different notions, but on the restricted language of Dung's frameworks, the notions coincide:

Proposition (6)

Let Δ be a Dung theory. Then a Δ-argument is dialectically justifying with respect to Δ if, and only if, it is admissible with respect to Δ.

Proof: Dialectically justifying arguments are always admissible. (This does not depend on Δ being a Dung theory.) Now let C be an admissible argument, and let C' be an argument incompatible with C. Since C and C' consist of Dung sentences, the incompatibility of C and C' implies that C attacks C' or that C' attacks C. In case C' attacks C, also C attacks C' since C is admissible. This shows that C is dialectically justifying.
Note that by this result the theorems on the extension existence and multiplicity problems can *for Dung theories* be rephrased in terms of admissibility instead of dialectical justification. This is not the case for theories in general. Then the notion of dialectical justification is essential. The key point is that admissibility does not have all of the properties used in the proof of the main theorem on the existence and multiplicity of dialectical interpretations. These properties are localization, union and separation at the base.

Their analogues for admissibility can be found by replacing 'dialectically justifying' by 'admissible' in the formulation of the properties. For instance, the union property (for pairs of arguments) for admissibility reads thus: if C and C' are compatible arguments, that are admissible with respect to a theory Δ, then also C ∪ C' is admissible with respect to the theory. Separation at the base becomes (again for pairs of arguments): if C and C' are incompatible arguments, that are admissible with respect to a theory Δ, then there are opposites φ and ψ in the theory, such that C supports φ and C' supports ψ.

It is not difficult to see that admissibility has the localization and union properties, but lacks the property of separation at the base.

For instance, that for admissibility, the property of separation at the base does not hold, can be seen by inspecting the theory $\{p_1, p_1 \leadsto q, p_2, p_2 \leadsto (q \leadsto \times q)\}$. With respect to this theory, there are four admissible arguments with a maximum number of elements, viz., each three-element subset of the theory. (Note that each argument of the theory is admissible since there are no attacking arguments.) Any pair of these arguments is incompatible, yet there is no sentence that is defeated by an argument, let alone by an admissible argument, as is required by the property of separation at the base.

It follows straightforwardly that the localization property obtains for admissibility: since, when E is an extension of a theory Δ, J(E) ∩ Δ is dialectically justifying with respect to Δ, J(E) ∩ Δ is certainly admissible.

The proof of the union property for admissibility is almost trivial since any attack on the union of a collection of arguments is also an attack on one of the arguments in the collection.

Inspection of the proof of the main theorem (3) shows that the property of separation at the base is only used in the 'if'-part. The 'only if'-part indeed has an analogue for admissibility since it only uses localization and union. The theory $\{p_1, p_1 \leadsto q, p_2, p_2 \leadsto (q \leadsto \times q)\}$ (the counterexample against the property of separation at the base) shows that the analogue of the 'if'-part is in fact not true. All sentences in the theory are 'admissibly justifiable', i.e., supported by an admissible argument, since any argument of the theory is admissible. No sentence in the theory is 'admissibly defeasible', i.e., attacked by an admissible argument, since there is no attacking argument at all. Still, the theory has no extension.

Verheij (2000a) expands this meta-analysis for other results (e.g., concerning so-called dialectically preferred and admissibly preferred arguments, i.e., those dialectically justifying or admissible arguments that are maximal with respect to set inclusion) and for other notions that are similar to dialectical justification.

Bondarenko et al. (1997) have used admissibility in their discussion of an abstract, argumentation-theoretic approach to default reasoning. Their setting, just as Dung's (1995), is related to DEFLOG's, yet they focus on deductive systems. Interestingly, whereas in DEFLOG dialectical negation × is treated as an ordinary connective, Bondarenko et al. consider the question of which sentences are contrary to others as part of the domain theory (as the mapping from sentences to their contraries is explicitly represented in their assumption-based frameworks). It seems that the notion of dialectical justification can be directly transplanted to their system. For the reasons discussed here and in the section on the existence and multiplicity of extensions, it can be expected that dialectical justification has better properties for analyzing assumption-based frameworks than admissibility.

LITERATURE

ALEVEN, V. (1997). *Teaching Case-Based Argumentation Through a Model and Examples*. Ph.D. Dissertation University of Pittsburgh.

ALEVEN, V. and ASHLEY, K.D. (1994). An instructional environment for practising argumentation skills. *Proceedings of the Twelfth National Conference on Artificial Intelligence*, Vol. 1, pp. 485-492. Seattle (Washington).

ASHLEY, K.D. (1990). *Modeling legal argument. Reasoning with cases and hypotheticals*. The MIT Press, Cambridge (Massachusetts).

ASSER-HARTKAMP (1998). *Mr. C. Asser's handleiding tot de beoefening van het Nederlands burgerlijk recht. Verbintenissenrecht. Deel III. De verbintenis uit de wet. Tiende druk bewerkt door Mr. A.S. Hartkamp.* Tjeenk Willink, Zwolle.

BARWISE, J. and ETCHEMENDY, J. (2000). *Language, Proof, and Logic*. Seven Bridges Press, New York (New York).

BELL, P. (1997). Using argument representations to make thinking visible for individuals and groups. *Proceedings of CSCL '97: The Second International Conference on Computer Support for Collaborative Learning* (eds. R. Hall, N. Miyake and N. Enyedy), pp. 10-19. University of Toronto Press, Toronto.

BENCH-CAPON, T.J.M. (1997). Argument in Artificial Intelligence and Law. *Artificial Intelligence and Law,* Vol. 5, pp. 249-261.

BENCH-CAPON, T.J.M., DUNNE, P.E.S. and LENG, P.H. (1991). Interacting with Knowledge Based Systems through Dialogue Games. *Proceedings of Eleventh International Conference, Expert Systems and their Applications*, Vol. 1, Avignon.

BENCH-CAPON, T.J.M., LENG, P.H. and STANIFORD, G. (1998). A Computer Supported Environment for the Teaching of Legal Argument. *Journal of Information, Law and Technology (JILT)*, No. 3. See <elj.warwick.ac.uk/jilt/98-3/capon.html>.

BENCH-CAPON, T.J.M. and SARTOR, G. (2001). Theory Based Explanation of Case Law Domains. *The 8th International Conference on Artificial Intelligence and Law. Proceedings of the Conference*, pp. 12-21. ACM, New York (New York).

BONDARENKO, A., DUNG, P.M., KOWALSKI, R.A. and TONI, F. (1997). An abstract, argumentation-theoretic approach to default reasoning. *Artificial Intelligence,* Vol. 93, pp. 63-101.

BOUWER, A. (1999). ArgueTrack: Computer Support for Educational Argumentation. *Analysing Educational Dialogue Interaction (AIED '99 Workshop 3)*, pp. 1-8.

BROUWER, P.W. (1990). *Samenhang in recht. Een analytische studie.* Wolters-Noordhoff, Groningen.

CHESÑEVAR, C.I., MAGUITMAN, A.G. and LOUI, R.P. (2000). Logical models of argument. *ACM Computing Surveys,* Vol. 32, No. 4, pp. 337-383.

CROMBAG, H.F.M., VAN KOPPEN, P.J. and WAGENAAR, W.A. (1994). *Dubieuze zaken: De psychologie van strafrechtelijk bewijs.* Contact, Amsterdam.

DUNG, P.M. (1993). On the acceptability of arguments and its fundamental role in nonmonotonic reasoning and logic programming. *IJCAI-93. Proceedings of the Thirteenth International Joint Conference on Artificial Intelligence* (ed. R. Bajcsy), pp. 852-857. Morgan Kaufmann Publishers, San Mateo (California).

DUNG, P.M. (1995). On the acceptability of arguments and its fundamental role in nonmonotonic reasoning, logic programming and n-person games. *Artificial Intelligence,* Vol. 77, pp. 321-357.

GABBAY, D.M., HOGGER, C.J. and ROBINSON, J.A. (eds.) (1994). *Handbook of Logic in Artificial Intelligence and Logic Programming. Volume 3. Nonmonotonic Reasoning and Uncertain Reasoning.* Clarendon Press, Oxford.

GAMUT, L.T.F. (1991). *Logic, Language, and Meaning. Volume I. Introduction to Logic.* The University of Chicago Press, Chicago.

GELFOND, M. and LIFSCHITZ, V. (1988). The stable model semantics for logic programming. *Logic Programming. Proceedings of the Fifth International Conference and Symposium* (eds. R.A. Kowalski and K.A. Bowen), pp. 1070-1080. The MIT Press, Cambridge (Massachusetts).

GORDON, T.F. (1994). The Pleadings game: An Exercise in Computational Dialectics. *Artificial Intelligence and Law,* Vol. 2, No. 4, pp. 239-292.

GORDON, T.F. (1996). Computational Dialectics. *Computers as Assistants. A New Generation of Support Systems* (ed. P. Hoschka), pp. 187-203. Lawrence Erlbaum Associates, Mahwah (New Jersey).

GORDON, T.F., JOHNIGK, S., SCHMIDT-BELZ, B., VOSS, A. and PETERSEN, U. (1999). Distance Learning Applications of the Zeno Mediation System.

Computer-Supported Collaborative Argumentation for Learning Communities Workshop at CSCL '99. See <kmi.open.ac.uk/sbs/csca/cscl99/>.

GORDON, T.F. and KARACAPILIDIS, N. (1997). The Zeno Argumentation Framework. *The Sixth International Conference on Artificial Intelligence and Law. Proceedings of the Conference*, pp. 10-18. ACM, New York (New York).

GORDON, T.F., VOSS, A., RICHTER, G. and MÄRKER, O. (2001). Zeno: Groupware for Discourses on the Internet. *Künstliche Intelligenz,* Vol. 2, pp. 43-45.

HAENNI, R., KOHLAS, J. and LEHMANN, N. (2001). Probabilistic Argumentation Systems. *Handbook of Defeasible Reasoning and Uncertainty Management Systems, Volume 5: Algorithms for Uncertainty and Defeasible Reasoning* (eds. J. Kohlas and S. Moral), pp. 221-288. Kluwer, Dordrecht.

HAGE, J.C. (1997). *Reasoning with Rules. An Essay on Legal Reasoning and Its Underlying Logic*. Kluwer Academic Publishers, Dordrecht.

HAGE, J.C. (2000). Dialectical Models in artificial intelligence and law. *Artificial Intelligence and Law,* Vol. 8, pp. 137-172.

HAGE, J.C. (2001a). Formalizing legal coherence. *The 8th International Conference on Artificial Intelligence and Law. Proceedings of the Conference*, pp. 22-31. ACM, New York (New York).

HAGE, J.C. (2001b). Legal logic. Its existence, nature and use. *Pluralism and Law* (ed. A. Soeteman), pp. 347-373. Kluwer Academic Publishers, Dordrecht.

HAGE, J.C., LEENES, R.E. and LODDER, A.R. (1994). Hard Cases: A Procedural Approach. *Artificial Intelligence and Law,* Vol. 2, pp. 113-167.

HUNTER, A. (2001). Hybrid argumentation systems for structured news reports. *Knowledge Engineering Review,* Vol. 16, pp. 295-329.

KARACAPILIDIS, N. and PADADIAS, D. (2001). Computer supported argumentation and collaborative decision making: the HERMES system. *Information Systems,* Vol. 26, pp. 259-277.

KOWALSKI, R.A. and TONI, F. (1996). Abstract Argumentation. *Artificial Intelligence and Law,* Vol. 4, pp. 275-296.

LEENES, R.E. (1998). *Hercules of Karneades. Hard cases in recht en rechtsinformatica*. Twente University Press, Enschede.

LODDER, A.R. (1998). *DiaLaw – on legal justification and dialog games*. Dissertation Universiteit Maastricht.

LODDER, A.R. and HUYGEN, P.E.M. (2001). eADR: A simple tool to structure the information exchange between parties in Online Dispute Resolution. *Legal Knowledge and Information Systems. JURIX 2001: The Fourteenth Annual Conference* (eds. B. Verheij, A.R. Lodder, R.P. Loui and A.J. Muntjewerff), pp. 117-119. IOS Press, Amsterdam.

LODDER, A.R. and VERHEIJ, B. (1998). Opportunities of computer-mediated legal argument in education. *Proceedings of the BILETA-conference – March 27-28*, Dublin, Ireland.

LOUI, R.P., NORMAN, J., ALTEPETER, J., PINKARD, D., CRAVEN, D., LINSDAY, J. and FOLTZ, M. (1997). Progress on Room 5. A Testbed for Public Interactive Semi-Formal Legal Argumentation. *The Sixth International Conference on Artificial Intelligence and Law. Proceedings of the Conference*, pp. 207-214. ACM, New York (New York).

MACCRIMMON, M. and TILLERS, P. (eds.) (2002). *The Dynamics of Judicial Proof. Computation, Logic, and Common Sense*. Physica-Verlag, Heidelberg.

MARSHALL, C.C. (1989). Representing the structure of a legal argument. *The Second International Conference on Artificial Intelligence and Law. Proceedings of the Conference*, pp. 121-127. ACM, New York (New York).

MAUDET, N. and MOORE, D.J. (1999). Dialogue Games for Computer Supported Collaborative Argumentation. *Computer Supported Collaborative Argumentation Workshop at CSCL '99*, Palo Alto. See <kmi.open.ac.uk/people/sbs/csca/cscl99/>.

MOMMERS, L. (2002). *Applied legal epistemology. Building a knowledge-based ontology of the legal domain.* Dissertation Leiden University.

MUNTJEWERFF, A.J. (2001). *An Instructional Environment for Learning to Solve Legal Cases. PROSA.* Dissertation Universiteit van Amsterdam.

NUTE, D. (1988). Defeasible reasoning: a philosophical analysis in Prolog. *Aspects of Artificial Intelligence* (ed. J.H. Fetzer), pp. 251-288. Kluwer Academic Publishers, Dordrecht.

PAOLUCCI, M., SUTHERS, D. and WEINER, A. (1996). Automated Advice-Giving Strategies for Scientific Inquiry. *Intelligent Tutoring Systems, Third International Conference, ITS '96. Montréal, Canada, June 12-14, 1996* (eds. C. Frasson, G. Gauthier and A. Lesgold), pp. 372-381. Springer Verlag, Berlin.

PECZENIK, A. (1989). *On Law and Reason*. Kluwer Academic Publishers, Dordrecht.

PECZENIK, A. and HAGE, J.C. (2000). Legal knowledge about what? *Ratio Juris,* Vol. 13, pp. 325-345.

POLLOCK, J.L. (1986). *Contemporary Theories of Knowledge*. Rowman and Littlefield, Totowa (New Jersey).

POLLOCK, J.L. (1987). Defeasible reasoning. *Cognitive Science,* Vol. 11, pp. 481-518.

POLLOCK, J.L. (1995). *Cognitive Carpentry: A Blueprint for How to Build a Person*. The MIT Press, Cambridge (Massachusetts).

PRAKKEN, H. (1993). *Logical tools for modelling legal argument.* Dissertation Vrije Universiteit Amsterdam.

PRAKKEN, H. (1997). *Logical Tools for Modelling Legal Argument. A Study of Defeasible Reasoning in Law*. Kluwer Academic Publishers, Dordrecht.

PRAKKEN, H., REED, C. and WALTON, D.N. (2003). Argumentation Schemes and Generalisations in Reasoning about Evidence. *The Ninth International Conference on Artificial Intelligence and Law. Proceedings of the Conference,* pp. 32-41. ACM, New York (New York).

PRAKKEN, H. and SARTOR, G. (1996). A Dialectical Model of Assessing Conflicting Arguments in Legal Reasoning. *Artificial Intelligence and Law,* Vol. 4, pp. 331-368.

PRAKKEN, H. and SARTOR, G. (1998). Modelling Reasoning with Precedents in a Formal Dialogue Game. *Artificial Intelligence and Law,* Vol. 6, pp. 231-287.

PRAKKEN, H. and VREESWIJK, G.A.W. (2002). Logics for Defeasible Argumentation. *Handbook of Philosophical Logic, Second Edition* (eds. D.M. Gabbay and F. Guenthner), Vol. 4, pp. 218-319. Kluwer Academic Publishers, Dordrecht.

RANNEY, M. and SCHANK, P. (1998). Modeling, observing, and promoting the explanatory coherence of social reasoning. *Connectionist and PDP models of social reasoning* (eds. S. Read and L. Miller), pp. 245-274. Lawrence Erlbaum Associates, Hillsdale (New Jersey).

REED, C. and WALTON, D.N. (2001). Applications of Argumentation Schemes. *Argumentation and its Applications. Proceedings of the Fourth Biennial Conference of the Ontario Society for the Study of Argumentation (OSSA 2001)* (eds. H.V. Hansen, C.W. Tindale, J.A. Blair and R.H. Johnson).

REHG, W., MCBURNEY, P. and PARSONS, S. (2001). Computer Decision-Support Systems for Public Argumentation: Philosophical Issues in

Deployment and Evaluation. *Argumentation and its Applications. Proceedings of the Fourth Biennial Conference of the Ontario Society for the Study of Argumentation (OSSA 2001)* (eds. H.V. Hansen, C.W. Tindale, J.A. Blair and R.H. Johnson).

REITER, R. (1980). A Logic for Default Reasoning. *Artificial Intelligence,* Vol. 13, pp. 81-132.

REITER, R. (1987). A Logic for Default Reasoning. *Readings in Nonmonotonic Reasoning* (ed. M.L. Ginsberg), pp. 68-93. Morgan Kaufmann Publishers, Los Altos (California). Reprinted from Reiter (1980).

REITER, R. and CRISCUOLO, G. (1981). On interacting defaults. *Proceedings of the Seventh International Joint Conference on Artificial Intelligence (IJCAI 81)*, pp. 270-276. Morgan Kaufmann Publishers, Los Altos (California).

REITER, R. and CRISCUOLO, G. (1987). On interacting defaults. *Readings in Nonmonotonic Reasoning* (ed. M.L. Ginsberg), pp. 94-100. Morgan Kaufmann Publishers, Los Altos (California). Reprinted from Reiter and Criscuolo (1981).

RETALIS, S., PAIN, H. and HAGGITH, M. (1996). Arguing with the Devil: Teaching in Controversial Domains. *Intelligent Tutoring Systems, Third International Conference, ITS '96, Montréal, Canada, June 12-14, 1996* (eds. C. Frasson, G. Gauthier and A. Lesgold), Springer-Verlag, Berlin.

RITTEL, H.W.J. and WEBBER, M.M. (1973). Dilemmas in a general theory of planning. *Policy Sciences,* Vol. 4.

ROLF, B. and MAGNUSSON, C. (2002). Developing the art of argumentation. A software approach. *5th International Conference on Argumentation (ISSA 2002)*, Amsterdam.

ROTH, A.C. (2003). *Case-based reasoning in the law. A formal theory of reasoning by case comparison.* Dissertation Universiteit Maastricht.

RUITER, D.W.P. (1993). *Institutional Legal Facts. Legal Powers and their Effects.* Kluwer Academic Publishers, Dordrecht.

SCHANK, P. (1995). *Computational tools for modeling and aiding reasoning: Assessing and applying the Theory of Explanatory Coherence.* Dissertation University of California, Berkeley.

SIMARI, G.R. and LOUI, R.P. (1992). A mathematical treatment of defeasible reasoning and its applications. *Artificial Intelligence,* Vol. 53, pp. 125-157.

SOETEMAN, A. (1989). *Logic in Law.* Kluwer Academic Publishers, Dordrecht.

SPAN, G. (2000). An Intelligent Tool for Acquiring Legal Case Solving Skills. *Rationality, Information and Progress in Law and Psychology. Liber Amicorum Hans F. Crombag* (eds. P.J. van Koppen and N. Roos), pp. 185-202. Metajuridica Publications, Maastricht.

SPIER, J., HARTLIEF, T., VAN MAANEN, G.E. and VRIESENDORP, R.D. (1997). *Verbintenissen uit de wet en Schadevergoeding*. Kluwer, Deventer.

STRANIERI, A. and ZELEZNIKOW, J. (2000). Argumentation Structures for Knowledge Management. *Proceedings of the Third International Conference on the Practical Applications of Knowledge Management PAKeM-2000*, pp. 51-69. The Practical Application Company, Blackpool.

SUTHERS, D. (1999). Representational Support for Collaborative Inquiry. *Proceedings of the 32nd Hawaii International Conference on the System Sciences (HICSS-32)*, Institute of Electrical and Electronics Engineers (IEEE).

SUTHERS, D. and WEINER, A. (1995). Groupware for Developing Critical Discussion Skills. *Proceedings of CSCL '95: the First International Conference on Computer Support for Collaborative Learning* (eds. J.L. Schnase and E.L. Cunnius), pp. 341-348. Lawrence Erlbaum Associates, Mahwah (New Jersey).

SUTHERS, D., WEINER, A., CONNELLY, J. and PAOLUCCI, M. (1995). Belvedere: Engaging Students in Critical Discussion of Science and Public Policy Issues. *Proceedings of the 7th World Conference on Artificial Intelligence in Education (AIED '95)*, pp. 266-273. Washington.

THAGARD, P. (1992). *Conceptual revolutions*. Princeton University Press, Princeton (New Jersey).

TOTH, J., SUTHERS, D. and WEINER, A. (1997). Providing Expert Advice in the Domain of Collaborative Scientific Inquiry. *8th World Conference on Artificial Intelligence in Education (AIED '97)*.

TOULMIN, S.E. (1958). *The uses of argument*. University Press, Cambridge.

VAN DALEN, D. (1983). *Logic and Structure. Second Edition*. Springer-Verlag, Berlin.

VAN EEMEREN, F.H., GROOTENDORST, R. and KRUIGER, T. (1981). *Argumentatietheorie*. Uitgeverij Het Spectrum, Utrecht.

VAN EEMEREN, F.H., GROOTENDORST, R. and KRUIGER, T. (1987). *Handbook of Argumentation Theory. A Critical Survey of Classical Backgrounds and Modern Studies*. Foris Publications, Dordrecht. Translation of van Eemeren et al. (1981).

van Gelder, T.J. (2001). The Reason! Project. *The Skeptic,* Vol. 21, No. 2, pp. 9-12.

Veerman, A. (2000). Computer-supported collabrative argumentation through argumentation. Dissertation Universiteit Utrecht.

Verheij, B. (1996a). *Rules, Reasons, Arguments. Formal studies of argumentation and defeat.* Dissertation Universiteit Maastricht. See <www.ai.rug.nl/~verheij/publications/proefschrift/>.

Verheij, B. (1996b). Two approaches to dialectical argumentation: admissible sets and argumentation stages. *NAIC '96. Proceedings of the Eighth Dutch Conference on Artificial Intelligence* (eds. J.-J.Ch. Meyer and L.C. van der Gaag), pp. 357-368. Universiteit Utrecht, Utrecht. A preliminary version was presented at the Computational Dialectics Workshop at FAPR-96. June 3-7, 1996, Bonn.

Verheij, B. (1998a). Argue! – an implemented system for computer-mediated defeasible argumentation. *NAIC '98. Proceedings of the Tenth Netherlands/Belgium Conference on Artificial Intelligence* (eds. H. La Poutré and H.J. van den Herik), pp. 57-66. CWI, Amsterdam.

Verheij, B. (1998b). ArguMed – A Template-Based Argument Mediation System for Lawyers. *Legal Knowledge Based Systems. JURIX: The Eleventh Conference* (eds. J.C. Hage, T.J.M. Bench-Capon, A.W. Koers, C.N.J. de Vey Mestdagh and C.A.F.M. Grütters), pp. 113-130. Gerard Noodt Instituut, Nijmegen.

Verheij, B. (1999a). Automated Argument Assistance for Lawyers. *The Seventh International Conference on Artificial Intelligence and Law. Proceedings of the Conference*, pp. 43-52. ACM, New York (New York).

Verheij, B. (1999b). Logic, context and valid inference. Or: Can there be a logic of law? *Legal Knowledge Based Systems. JURIX 1999: The Twelfth Conference* (eds. H.J. van den Herik, M.-F. Moens, J. Bing, B. van Buggenhout, J. Zeleznikow and C.A.F.M. Grütters), pp. 109-121. Gerard Noodt Instituut, Nijmegen.

Verheij, B. (2000a). DEFLOG – a logic of dialectical justification and defeat. Manuscript. See <www.ai.rug.nl/~verheij/publications/DefLog15.htm>.

Verheij, B. (2000b). Dialectical Argumentation as a Heuristic for Courtroom Decision Making. *Rationality, Information and Progress in Law and Psychology. Liber Amicorum Hans F. Crombag* (eds. P.J. van Koppen and N. Roos), pp. 203-226. Metajuridica Publications, Maastricht.

Verheij, B. (2001a). Evaluating arguments based on Toulmin's scheme. *Argumentation and its Applications. Proceedings of the Fourth Biennial Conference of the Ontario Society for the Study of Argumentation (OSSA 2001)* (eds. H.V. Hansen, C.W. Tindale, J.A. Blair and R.H. Johnson).

Verheij, B. (2001b). Legal decision making as dialectical theory construction with argumentation schemes. *The 8th International Conference on Artificial Intelligence and Law. Proceedings of the Conference*, pp. 225-226. ACM, New York (New York).

Verheij, B. (2003a). DefLog: on the logical interpretation of prima facie justified assumptions. *Journal of Logic and Computation,* Vol. 13, No. 3, pp. 319-346.

Verheij, B. (2003b). Artificial argument assistants for defeasible argumentation. *Artificial Intelligence,* Vol. 150, No. 1-2, pp. 291-324.

Verheij, B., Hage, J.C. and van Maanen, G.E. (1999). De logica van de onrechtmatige daad. *Nederlands Tijdschrift voor Burgerlijk Recht,* Vol. 16, No. 4, pp. 95-102.

Vreeswijk, G.A.W. (1995). IACAS: an Implementation of Chisholm's Principles of Knowledge. *Dutch/German Workshop on Nonmonotonic Reasoning. Proceedings of the Second Workshop*, pp. 225-234. Delft University of Technology, Universiteit Utrecht.

Vreeswijk, G.A.W. (1997). Abstract argumentation systems. *Artificial Intelligence,* Vol. 90, pp. 225-279.

Wagenaar, W.A., van Koppen, P.J. and Crombag, H.F.M. (1993). *Anchored Narratives. The Psychology of Criminal Evidence.* Harvester Wheatsheaf, London.

Walton, D.N. (1996). *Argument Schemes for Presumptive Reasoning.* Lawrence Erlbaum Associates, Mahwah (New Jersey).

Walton, D.N. (1998). *The New Dialectic: Conversational Contexts of Argument.* University of Toronto Press, Toronto.

Walton, D.N. and Krabbe, E. (1995). *Commitment in Dialogue. Basic Concepts of Interpersonal Reasoning.* State University of New York Press, Albany (New York).

WEB ADDRESSES

All addresses were successfully visited in August, 2004.

Araucaria
<www.computing.dundee.ac.uk/staff/creed/research/araucaria.html>
Argue! and the ArguMed systems
<www.rechten.unimaas.nl/metajuridica/verheij/aaa/>
Athena
<www.athenasoft.org>
Belvedere (applet version)
<lilt.ics.Hawaii.edu/lilt/software/belvedere/applet.html>
Computer-Supported Collaborative Argumentation Resource Site
<kmi.open.ac.uk/people/sbs/csca/>
Concince Me
<dewey.soe.berkeley.edu/~schank/convinceme/>
Conflict resolution web site
<www.mediate.com>
GeNIe
<www2.sis.pitt.edu/~genie/>
Hermes
<www-sop.inria.fr/aid/hermes/>
Logic animations
<turing.wins.uva.nl/~jaspars/animations/>
MarshalPlan
<tillers.net/marshal.html>
Nathan
<www.cs.wustl.edu/~loui/natnathan.text>
Oscar
<www.u.arizona.edu/~pollock/oscar.html>
Reason!Able
<www.goreason.com>
Resources on case management and litigation support
<www.digital-lawyer.com/digital-lawyer/resource/caseman.html>

Room 5
<www.cs.wustl.edu/~room5/>
The Reason! project
<www.philosophy.unimelb.edu.au/reason/>
Weblog about computer-supported governance and democracy
<www.tfgordon.de>
Wise, including KIE's SenseMaker
<wise.berkeley.edu>
Workshop on Computer-Supported Collaborative Argumentation for Learning Communities
<kmi.open.ac.uk/people/sbs/csca/cscl99/>
Workshop on online dispute resolution at ICAIL 2003
<www.odrworkshop.org>
Zeno
<zeno.fhg.de>

INDEX

INFORMATION TECHNOLOGY & LAW SERIES

1. E-Government and its Implications for Administrative Law – Regulatory Initiatives in France, Germany, Norway and the United States (The Hague: T·M·C·ASSER PRESS, 2002)
   Editor: J.E.J. Prins / ISBN 90-6704-141-6
2. Digital Anonymity and the Law – Tensions and Dimensions (The Hague: T·M·C·ASSER PRESS, 2003)
   Editors: C. Nicoll, J.E.J. Prins and M.J.M. van Dellen / ISBN 90-6704-156-4
3. Protecting the Virtual Commons – Self-Organizing Open Source and Free Software Communities and Innovative Intellectual Property Regimes (The Hague: T·M·C·ASSER PRESS, 2003)
   Authors: R. van Wendel de Joode, J.A. de Bruijn and M.J.G. van Eeten / ISBN 90-6704-159-9
4. IT Support and the Judiciary – Australia, Singapore, Venezuela, Norway, The Netherlands and Italy (The Hague: T·M·C·ASSER PRESS, 2004)
   Editors: A. Oskamp, A.R. Lodder and M. Apistola / ISBN 90-6704-168-8
5. Electronic Signatures – Authentication Technology from a Legal Perspective (The Hague: T·M·C·ASSER PRESS, 2004)
   Author: M.H.M. Schellekens / ISBN 90-6704-174-2
6. Virtual Arguments – On the Design of Argument Assistants for Lawyers and Other Arguers (The Hague: T·M·C·ASSER PRESS, 2004)
   Author: B. Verheij / ISBN 90-6704-190-4

MIX
Papier aus verantwortungsvollen Quellen
Paper from responsible sources
FSC® C105338

If you have any concerns about our products,
you can contact us on
ProductSafety@springernature.com

In case Publisher is established outside the EU,
the EU authorized representative is:
Springer Nature Customer Service Center GmbH
Europaplatz 3, 69115 Heidelberg, Germany

Printed by Libri Plureos GmbH
in Hamburg, Germany